BEST OF BRITISH

Best of British is published by Patrick Stephens Ltd, Bar Hill, Cambridge, CB3 8EL, in conjunction with EMAP National Publications Ltd, 21 Church Walk, Peterborough.
Printed in Great Britain by Hazell Watson and Viney, Aylesbury. Set and composed by Mallard Studios, Peterborough. Colour process by Woolthame Ltd, London.
© 1979 EMAP National Publications Ltd.
All rights reserved. No part of this publication may be reproduced, stored in a retrieval system, or transmitted, in any form or by any means, electronic, mechanical, photo-copying, recording or otherwise, without prior permission, in writing from EMAP National Publications Ltd and Patrick Stephens Ltd.
First published in 1979
ISBN 0 - 85059 - 409 - X

Contents

4 — 5	Introduction
6 — 15	The British Industry
16 — 19	AJS 500 Springtwin
20 — 23	Ariel WD 350
24 — 27	Ariel VB
28 — 31	Ariel Huntmaster
32 — 35	Ariel Square Four
36 — 39	Ariel Leader
40 — 43	BSA 350 B31
44 — 47	BSA B40 SS90
48 — 51	BSA Bantam D1
52 — 55	BSA Golden Flash
56 — 59	BSA Gold Star
60 — 63	BSA Rocket Gold Star
64 — 67	BSA Fury 350
68 — 71	Douglas 350 MK V
72 — 73	Francis Barnett Cruiser
74 — 75	Greeves Sport
76 — 77	James Captain
78 — 81	Matchless G3LS
82 — 85	Norton ES2
86 — 87	Norton Jubilee
88 — 91	Norton International
92 — 95	Norton SS 650
96 — 99	Norton Dominator 88
100 — 103	Panther 100
104 — 105	Royal Enfield Crusader
106 — 109	Royal Enfield Bullet
110 — 113	Royal Enfield Meteor Minor
114 — 117	Scott Flying Squirrel
118 — 121	Sunbeam S7
122 — 125	Triumph TR5
126 — 129	Triumph Tiger 100A
130 — 133	Triumph Tiger 110
134 — 135	Triumph Tiger Cub
136 — 139	Velocette Vogue
140 — 143	Velocette Thruxton
144 — 147	Vincent HRD Rapide
148 — 151	Vincent Black Shadow
152 — 155	Vincent Comet 500
156 — 158	Owners' Clubs

Introduction

**by Peter Howdle
Associate Editor
Motor Cycle News**

ALL good things come to an end but the conclusion of the Best of British series in Motor Cycle News was lamented by so many readers that it seemed only right and proper to reprint the articles in a book.

The original stories about British machines and their proud owners appeared in 1978. They were an instant success and it is no exaggeration to say that the series was the most popular in the history of the paper.

Most of the bikes were located in Northamptonshire. Indeed, there was a time when I toyed with the idea of localising the whole thing by tracking down examples of every leading make on my doorstep.

Only occasionally did it become necesary to explore further afield but it was inevitable that, whenever a bike appeared in print, another proud owner would claim to have an even better example!

Although originality of specification is the yardstick of the vintage specialist, only a few of the models featured with their owners were in mint condition. But nearly every bike was in running order when we saw it.

Some were truly classic specimens. Others were quite ordinary jobs salvaged from the scrap heap. A few could even be regarded by cynics as the Worst of British, yet all form part of a colourful tapestry which gives many folk a great deal of pleasure.

With the British motor cycle industry virtually extinct since 1975, even the most humble of the species has become tinged with the nostalgia of all our yesterdays.

At a time when a whole generation of motor cyclists have grown up with Japanese machines ruling the roost, all sorts of people have a golden excuse for collecting and playing with obsolete British bikes.

The majority are genuine enthusiasts with an intimate knowledge of their machines. Many get as much pleasure from restoring them as they do from riding them while others find a British bike a convenient form of investment.

Sadly, many bikes which a few years ago would have been written off because of their low trade-in value, have rocketed in price and become highly sought-after goodies with greater commercial prospects than some art treasures.

The writer has personal experience of most of the machines described and illustrated in this book but thanks are due to a number of people for their specialised knowledge and invaluable contributions.

Owners themselves proved extremely knowledgeable but former members of the British industry, notably Mick Bowers and Jack Harper of BSA, Sammy Miller and Clive Bennett of Ariel, Bob Collier of Norton, Ken Sprayson of Reynolds, Ivor Davies of Triumph, and Ted Davies of Vincent-HRD all came to the rescue with information.

Thanks are also due to Charlie Rous, Paul Fowler, Brian Tarbox and Terry Snelling who made valuable contributions to the series, and to the many readers whose constructive criticisms not only enabled us to winkle out some errors but also to include additional details.

Although it will not be long before early Japanese bikes acquire vintage status in their own right, this book is essentially a tribute to the enthusiasts who have dedicated their spare time to preserving or restoring the Best of British. Long may they ride 'em!

More like a club than an

THE PATRIOTISM of a Birmingham dealer waiting to welcome representatives of a leading Japanese factory may help to put the decline and collapse of the British industry into some kind of perspective.

Keen to give his guests a good impression, he ordered his showrooms to be cleaned and polished and for the rows of new and secondhand bikes to be bulled up like soldiers ready for inspection by the Queen.

On the morning of the visit, our worthy trader looked distinctly detuned. The floor under almost every British bike was stained with tell-tale droppings while their Japanese rivals remained disgustingly oil tight.

Then came the sort of inspiration that has always made Britain one of the most resourceful nations in the world. The artful dealer sent a boy out for a load of brand new baking tins and had one placed under each bike.

The dripping continued but, as zero hour arrived and the inscrutable visitors stepped out of their limousine to admire the exterior of the shop, the activity inside was quite incredible.

Dashing round like greased lightning, the dealer and his merry men switched all the tins round before greeting their bewildered visitors with cups of best of British tea. No names no pack drill! And no need to say which bikes had the most oil under them!

It was all good, clean, harmless fun. But although the visitors remained haughtily polite, they were plainly not amused.

Whether or not the case of the oily baking tins ever got back to Tokyo has never been ascertained but the incident happened just before bulldozers flattened the remains of the nearby BSA factory.

It was all over. Apart from a few isolated pockets of resistance, the British industry was extinct and some of the most glorious chapters in motor cycling had slipped into history.

But why? How come the British factories which were for so long the world's leading motor cycle producers could disintegrate so quickly? Was it lack of cash, complacency, mismanagement or just old age?

All these factors contributed to the downfall but it is all too easy to be wise after the event. Some experts say the rot started when control of the industry changed from the hands of the engineers into those of the accountants. The truth is that after years of struggling for survival, the British industry was killed off by political intrigue and Japanese competition.

The British industry had lasted about 75 years. It had survived many ups and downs but the odds were against it. Today, apart from a trickle of Triumphs and

Right: The sprawling industrial complex that once formed the heart of the BSA motor cycle empire, at Armoury Road, Small Heath, Birmingham.
Below left: Even the big bosses rode their products. Edward Turner, who designed the original 500 Triumph Speed Twin before World War 2, is pictured with a post-war version with the ill-fated bathtub back end. Hugh Palin, then secretary of the British Cycle and Motor Cycle Association, is behind the Triumph supremo during a press launch in the Welsh hills.
Below right: Dennis Poore with the MCN Machine of the Year trophy awarded to the Norton Commando. The machine was the last British bike to win the readers' popularity poll.

industry...

a handful of specialist machines, the industry is best remembered by the bikes which proud owners cherish as the Best of British.

While the back streets of Birmingham are no longer bustling with the activity that once made the city the hub of the world's biggest motor cycle producing country, the memories of those glorious years become more rosy as the years roll on.

Sadly, the Birmingham Motor Cycle Club headquarters, once frequented by practically every personality in the sport and industry, is also down for demolition. The passing of the wooden building they called the Motordrome is symbolic. For the British motor cycle manufacturing business was really more like a club than an industry.

That some of its greatest leaders, including Edward Turner, the autocratic but brilliant designer behind some of the finest examples of British machines, chose to dismiss the Japanese threat until it was too late is regrettable but true.

While the Japanese infiltration started in the 1960s, it took about ten years and the financial crash of the BSA empire in 1973 for westerners to realise the end was inevitable.

To salvage something from the BSA ruins, the government invited Dennis Poore, head of Norton Villiers since 1966, to form Norton Villiers Triumph in a bid to continue production of Triumph machines.

Despite a government investment of nearly £5 million, the new organisation was soon confronted by a succession of insoluble problems. By the end of 1975, production of Nortons at the old Villiers factory in Wolverhampton had come to a standstill and the plant was in the hands of the liquidator.

Triumph three cylinder models continued to be built in small batches at the old BSA factory, at Small Heath, Birmingham, but the place was in the hands of a receiver and manager appointed by the company's bankers.

It was an unhappy ending to a rescue operation which began in 1962 when Mr Poore and fellow directors of Manganese Bronze Holdings set out to restore the profit and loss accounts of ailing Associated Motor Cycles and Villiers Engineering companies.

By 1975, the former Triumph factory near Coventry had become a government sponsored workers cooperative. The set-up was strictly a manufacturing plant and the 750cc Bonneville twins it produced were sold through the marketing organisations of Norton Villiers Triumph. Even then, the future of the cooperative looked pretty shaky.

The future of the cooperative hinged on further

Bert Greeves, founder and managing director of a motor cycle factory which specialised in competition machines, tries a roadster version with a glass fibre sidecar.

The portals of the James factory where the author spent eight years as advertising manager. In the picture, left to right, are Garth Wheldon and Norman Moore, of the competition and development departments, and managing director Charles Sommerton. The bike is an ISDT works bike, with AMC engine and front hub.

government backing and the events of 1979, when mass sackings and the closure of a large part of the Meriden factory preceded yet another financial crisis, virtually put the lid on one of the last outposts of this proud industry.

Until the crunch at Meriden, the cooperative was making in the region of 300 bikes a week. Of these, only 20 per cent were for the home market. And the bulk of the 80 per cent which went for export was shipped to America, the market that kept the British industry in business long after it dived into the red.

From topsy-turvy beginnings at the turn of the century, Britain's motor cycle craftsmen rose to become the world's leaders in their field. For over 40 years, from the 1920s to the 1960s, British bikes and British riders were supreme in international sport.

The achievements of great racing men such as Geoff Duke, John Surtees, Bob McIntyre, Mike Hailwood and Phil Read, along with many more, were all part of a proud tapestry in which makes like AJS, Ariel, Brough Superior, BSA, Douglas, Excelsior, Francis Barnett, Greeves, James, Matchless, Norton, Panther, Royal Enfield, Rudge, Scott, Sunbeam, Triumph, Velocette and Vincent were respected wherever twistgrips were tweaked.

British manufacturers and riders won the International Six Days Trial more often than any other country. So much so that, although the ISDT World Trophy has eluded them since 1953, they have still won the top team contest more times than anybody.

Most pre-war world speed records were held by British riders and it was only in the late 1970s that their supremacy in trials and moto cross became eroded by Europeans and Americans.

Despite its impressive record, the British industry was never equipped for mass production. Not even BSA, the biggest of them all, could boast a high output from an assortment of old-fashioned factories with more in common with the industrial revolution of the 1880s than with 20th century motor cycling.

The original home of Norton, in Bracebridge Street, Birmingham, was an incredible labyrinth of workshops from which Norton became the greatest name in international racing for more than a quarter of a century.

Technicians like Joe Craig, Doug Hele and Bert Hopwood wielded tremendous influence and there was a certain magic about the Norton Inter and sidecar which told visitors that works manager Bill Stone was hard at it. But it is with mixed views that historians reflect on a 490cc single cylinder Norton which remained in production for 40 years with only detail improvements!

Only the better known makes have already been mentioned. There were in fact many more, notably Greeves who produced the machines on which Dave Bickers won Britain's last 250cc world moto cross title, in 1961, but their output was always small by Japanese standards.

When Britain's industry was at its peak, in the 1950s and 1960s, her factories churned out a total of

Gone for ever! Front of the AMC factory in Plumstead Road, Woolwich, once the proud headquarters of an empire which included the Matchless, Norton, AJS, James and Francis Barnett makes. AMC's closure in 1965 was the first major blow to Britain's bike industry.

250,000 motor cycles a year. Today, the Japanese giants have a total production of more than 4,000,000 units a year, Honda alone making five times as many bikes as Britain did in one year!

With brand new factories and up to date machine tools, following America's industrial rehabilitation of Japan after World War 2, the names of Honda, Yamaha, Suzuki and Kawasaki quickly became key words in motor cycling jargon.

As far back as the early 1960s, British lightweight motor cycle manufacturers faced overwhelming competition. While Francis Barnett and James continued to be powered by old-fashioned Villiers engines, Honda and Suzuki came out with faster and more efficient designs. The writing was on the wall.

There were a few notable exceptions, such as the 250 Ariel Leader introduced in 1958 with an engine based on the obsolete Adler. But the BSA Bantam, itself developed from a pre-war DKW following post-war reparations, had long reached the end of its popularity.

Britain's only hope was to concentrate on high performance machines which continued to appeal to the America market. The legendary Vincent Black Shadow, from a small factory at Stevenage, Hertfordshire, remained the world's fastest production motor cycle until well into the 1960s. But Vincents were always expensive, built for connoisseurs regardless of cost, and never a successful commercial proposition. Inevitably, the makers sought other outlets and the factory folded.

Without enormous capital investment, Britain's industry was doomed. Investors were not attracted and the first major blow came with the financial collapse of the Associated Motor Cycles group, in 1965.

The AMC organisation, which began with AJS and Matchless, had taken over the James, Francis Barnett and Norton factories in the late 1950s. Don Heather, then managing director, had dismissed Italy's fashionable Vespa and Lambretta scooters as novelties which would never catch on. Ironically, AMC launched a James scooter when the fashion was past its peak and it never caught on.

Well known for its 350cc AJS and 500cc Matchless overhead camshaft racing singles, and for the famous pushrod plonker of trials stars Hugh Viney and Gordon Jackson, the AMC group was based at Plumstead, London. It tried to keep up with the times with a major retooling programme and was forced into bankruptcy.

Three of the five makes under the AMC banner vanished overnight. Thanks to Dennis Poore, chairman of the Manganese Bronze Holdings group, AJS and Norton were to live a little longer. He formed Norton Villiers after acquiring the remains of AMC from the official receiver in 1966.

The take-over marked the debut of the 750 Norton Commando, a touring machine with the much-publicised Isolastic frame with massive rubber mountings to absorb the vibration of an extensively revamped but old-fashioned pushrod twin.

Douglas Bader (centre), the legless Battle of Britain fighter pilot, receives a 350 Matchless in cross-country trim for the first Outward Bound School. The bike was presented to the wartime hero and founder of the scheme by Jock West (right), former road racer and AMC sales chief who also served with the RAF during World War 2.

An historic moment as East Midland Allied Press chairman Mr R P W Winfrey presents the first Motor Cycle News Machine of the Year award to Ken Whistance, general manager of Ariel in 1958. The Ariel Leader won.

Reg Weeks, export manager of Norton Motors, with one of the Manx Norton singles which were for so long the world's most successful racing motor cycles. This Earls Court show specimen would be worth a mint today.

The AJS name was kept for moto cross machines produced in limited numbers for a few years. A former racing driver with a passionate interest in motor cycles and a great deal of patriotic drive, Mr Poore encouraged a competition department which achieved considerable success in production machine racing but never quite made the grade in moto cross.

Norton production was at the former Villiers works in Wolverhampton while a new home was found for an assembly plant and distribution centre at Andover, Hampshire.

It was a far cry from the days when Norton managing director Gilbert Smith personally cut the daily meat joint in the executive dining room and everyone had more time for racing heroes than for time and motion study whizz kids.

Other famous makes failed to find a saviour. The Ariel factory at Selly Oak, Birmingham, was already part of the BSA group before it closed in 1965. It folded at a time when Ken Whistance, one of the most dynamic of Britain's motor cycling supremos, was preparing to introduce a 750 in-line four with overhead camshaft and electric starter. The prototype is now privately owned.

The Royal Enfield brand collapsed in 1970. Originally based at Redditch, Worcestershire, the company changed hands several times before production was switched to Bradford on Avon, Wiltshire, where the massive 750cc Constellation was built in a former underground aircraft factory. The location eventually proved more profitable for growing mushrooms and the last batch of Enfield engines was sold to Rickman Engineering, of New Milton, Hants.

The Velocette factory, at Hall Green, Birmingham, folded in 1971. Despite taking on outside engineering contracts, including pressings for James, and

Clive Bennett (left), one of the key men at Ariel before the factory was absorbed into BSA, discusses a works BSA for the Daytona 200 miler with Alan Shepherd, one of the road racing stars during the golden fifties and sixties.

Above: One of the stalwarts of the BSA motor cycle division, home sales manager Fred Green, goes in for a spot of modelling during a motor cycle show in Brighton. The corduroys and boots, in colours to match the 750 Rocket triple, were part of a drive to repel the Japanese invasion.
Right: Triumph rolls again. The first machines to leave Meriden after a blockade by workers arrive at NVT's Waverley Road, Birmingham, depot in June 1974. About 2,500 bikes were locked in.

making engines for small hovercrafts, managing director Bertie Goodman was forced to close down and find employment with Norton Villiers. After spending a few years in Canada, he returned to NVT as design co-ordinator for a BSA Beaver with a 50cc Minarelli engine from Italy. Times do not always change for the better.

In the end, apart from small specialists making moto cross, road racing and trials machines, the British industry was down to the BSA-Triumph and Norton-Villiers groups. And despite a succession of economic problems, the BSA motor cycle division continued to thrive. Or so it seemed to the man in the street who envied BSA Testers with trade plates on their beautiful bikes.

Visitors to the Armoury Road headquarters were impressed with a modernisation scheme which involved an intricate conveyor system. Marketing experts travelled all over the world to try to compete with the Japanese. And exports boomed so impressively that, in 1966 and 1967, both BSA and Triumph were honoured with the Queen's Awards to Industry.

These achievements were inconsistent with the retirement in 1963 of Edward Turner as managing director of the company's motor cycle group. Creator of the pre-war 500cc Triumph Speed Twin, which formed the basis of the machines later produced by the Meriden cooperative, he was succeeded by Harry Sturgeon whose brilliant leadership restored the confidence of shareholders.

It was during his reign that Jeff Smith, riding BSA four-strokes with titanium frames, won the 500cc world moto cross championships, in 1964 and 1965. Tragically, Harry Sturgeon died of a brain tumour in 1967 and his successors unhappily failed to emulate his example.

Huge sums were wasted on ill-fated projects like the revival of the Ariel brand in 1970 for a BSA motorised shopping tricycle and profits took a sharp dive.

In 1971, company chairman Eric Turner (unrelated to Edward) announced a loss of £8,500,000. This compared with a record profit of £3,500,000 ten years before when he took over from Jack Sangster, who had originally sold the Triumph factory to BSA for £2,500,000 in 1951 and became a leading light in group affairs.

Intervention by the British government's Department of Trade and Industry saved the BSA group from bankruptcy. A healthy powered two-wheeler industry was regarded as vital to the national economy. And nearly half of the £10,000,000 capital with which Norton Villiers Triumph was founded in 1973 came from public funds.

The scheme was for NVT to develop a viable challenge, based on good solid British engineering, which would ultimately make a profit. The government loan was regarded as an investment and NVT enjoyed advantageous repayment terms.

The formation of NVT coincided with the enlargement of the Norton Commando from 750 to 850cc but the inescapable fact remained that the design was basically 25 years old. The Triumph Trident, originally launched in 1968, was more modern but many components of the 750cc three cylinder roadster were identical or near relatives of parts used in the firm's twin cylinder engines for over 30 years.

The Commando and the Trident faced formidable competition from Oriental and Continental superbikes. Their biggest rivals were the superbly reliable, albeit very vulnerable, Japanese multis, but Germany's luxurious BMW twins and Italy's rakish Benelli, Ducati, Guzzi and Laverda models all claimed a growing share of European and American sales.

With a trading loss running at nearly £4,000,000 a year, NVT announced the closure of Meriden's Triumph factory. The proposed sale of the factory was expected to yield about £5,000,000 which would boost the working capital for Triumph production in the old BSA factory in Birmingham.

Sadly, the plan meant the sacking of most of the 1,800 Triumph workers. And trade unions and local Labour MPs sparked off a political storm which probably killed any hope of the British industry surviving on a profitable basis.

Pickets prevented NVT management from entering the factory. Inside were some 4,000 complete and incomplete machines worth approximately £2,000,000. And the supply of Triumph spares dried up completely.

The sit-in by Triumph workers was illegal. It would have been expedient for NVT to bring in the police but Chris Chataway, the Minister who initiated the NVT scheme, urged the management to avoid a clash which might adverseley affect an imminent election. The Conservatives were already in hot water with the coal miners' union!

When the Conservatives lost the election, in 1974, and Tony Benn became the Labour government's new minister for industry, the Triumph workers were in clover. Under a government dedicated to nationalisation, they were encouraged to apply for government aid to form a cooperative.

In 1975, the government approved a loan of nearly £5,000,000. The workers cooperative was in business. Ironically, its formation coincided with a massive drop in bike sales in America.

Importers of Japanese machines offered huge discounts to clear warehouses bulging with unsold

13

superbikes. Unable to cut their prices, NVT chiefs told the government that a further massive cash injection was needed to bridge the gap until sales improved.

Politics knocked a few more nails into the coffin. A cabinet reshuffle gave Mr Benn's job to Eric Varley. And Mr Varley refused to approve any further government aid to the ailing motor cycle industry. Inevitably, NVT subsidiaries in Wolverhampton and Birmingham fell into the hands of official receivers.

New designs from NVT have yet to set the world on fire. The Norton Challenge, a 750cc ohc twin-cylinder machine designed by Keith Duckworth, of the Cosworth engineering organisation, failed to live up to the firm's Formula 1 car racing record.

Without the resources for making motor cycles, except on a very small scale, NVT pinned its future on a single rotor Norton-Wankel which took nearly ten years to develop before going into limited production at Shenstone, Warwickshire.

Providing sales of BSA mini-bikes with Minarelli engines reached 15,000 to 20,000 a year, the company could go ahead with plans to make their own engines at Garretts Green, Birmingham.

The firm assembles and markets 125 and 175cc street and off-road models with Yamaha engines in Italian frames, along with mopeds and children's garden bikes with Morini engines, while the Andover plant remains in business for BSA, Triumph and Norton spares in addition to Can-Am machines.

Experimental Norton-Wankel engine pictured in 1974. The project took ten years before going into limited production.

While Weslake engines made great strides into speedway, Lord Alexander Hesketh, of motor racing fame, quietly fostered a plan to produce an all-British machine powered by a 750cc Weslake vee-twin engine.

In 1978, when new motor cycle registrations in Britain were the highest for 20 years — the all-time record was 330,000 in 1959 — and clubs catering for owners of obsolete British machines were gaining more and more recruits, Lord Hesketh had no illusions of competing with the major factories.

If his Hesketh V-twin ever goes into production it could become a prestige machine in the tradition of the legendary George Brough. For although Mr Brough's output was no more than 3,000 machines in 20 years, his Brough Superiors were dubbed "The Rolls Royce of Motor Cycles" — probably the most prestigious slogan in the history of motor cycling and not even rivalled by the six-cylinder flagships from the Orient.

There were good British bikes and a few bad ones. Some leaked oil while others were so well put together that the gearbox casting remained permanently dry. Some vibrated more than others but, in general, British bikes had a lot going for them.

They were basically simple and easy to ride and maintain and most of them could survive being dropped or knocked over without breaking the bank. By modern standards, the heaviest of them was comparatively light.

It seems unlikely that the phoenix will arise from the ashes in the near future but nothing is impossible and it is comforting to know that, in addition to the die-hards of NVT and Triumph, several hundred members of the old BSA factory still work under the same roof.

At the helm of one of the NVT branches in the Midlands, former BSA works manager Alastair Cave runs a busy engineering plant, with its own foundry and loaded with machine tools, where apprentices are still given the opportunity of restoring old bikes whenever the chance arises.

The factory undertakes contract work for the motor industry, but the spirit of the British bike industry lives on. Only time will tell whether a revival is practical or not.

Happy days! Author Peter Howdle, in 'casual gear', tests a prototype James on the Mira pave back in 1954.

AJS 500 Springtwin

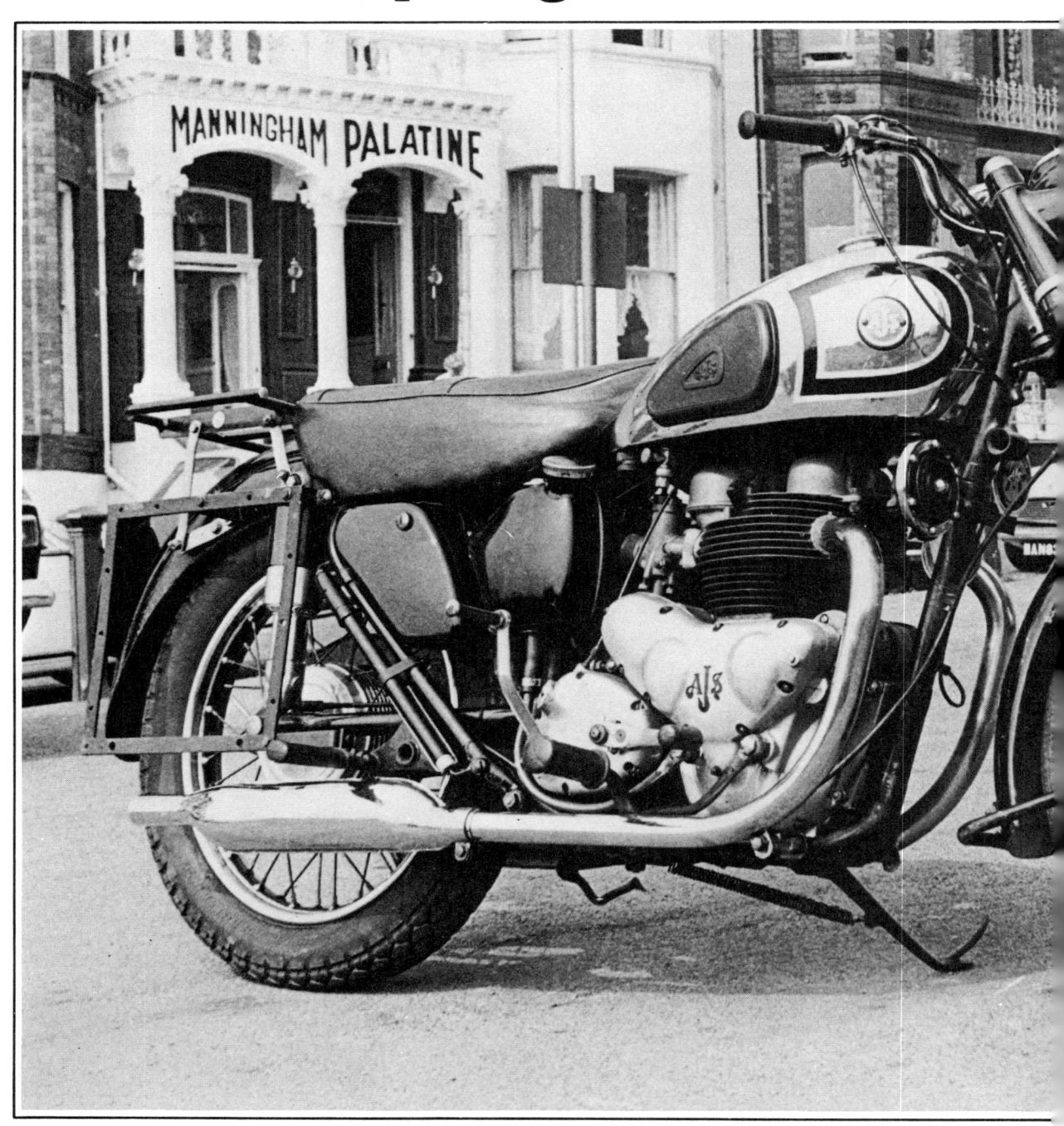

Stylish, comfortable, easy to maintain, but not particularly quick, the AJS or Matchless 500 Springtwins were splendid examples of the AMC factory's obsession for trying to make things better and, wherever possible, to make everything themselves.

While all other vertical twins got along very nicely with a two-bearing crankshaft and a common cylinder block, the AMC engines had a three-bearing crank and separate barrels under a common cylinder head.

The extra support improved the rigidity of the bottom end but this gain was offset by loss of rigidity at the top. And the design was further complicated by separate oil pumps for scavenging and delivery.

An oil distribution device was fitted to pressure feed individual components but the main effect of this unnecessary sophistication was to accentuate oil leaks in the best of British tradition!

Introduced in 1949 and originally for export only, the G9 Matchless and Model 20 AJS differed only in cosmetic details, the most remarkable being imitation megaphone silencers on the Matchbox.

Jock West, then sales director of the thriving Associated Motor Cycles Organisation at Plumstead Road, Woolwich, London, where both makes were built under the same roof, was largely responsible for tidying up the efforts of his drawing office.

A stickler for smooth contours, he made important contributions to styling which other makers blissfully ignored.

Neat front mudguard mounting-cum-valances and separate but extremely vulnerable car-type parking lights each side of the headlamp were typical AMC gimmicks of the mid 'fifties.

A more practical feature was a quickly detachable rear wheel, with a tommy bar on the spindle nut. This reflected the influence of works trials ace Hugh Viney, then a star member of a British ISDT team which won the World Trophy with devastating superiority.

Large alloy domes for the rocker box covers made tappet adjustment a doddle but pressure lubrication led to excessive wear in the valve guides and one of the worst components was a tin primary case secured by rubber and aluminium strips.

To give credit where it is due, AMC eventually replaced the tin case, which cunning owners sealed by injecting a spoonful of hot tallow, by one of the best alloy cases in the industry. They also realised the impracticability of making their own "jam pot" rear shockers and switched to Girling legs.

Luxurious upholstery and soft suspension made the Springtwin one of the most comfortable touring bikes of its time.

The alloy primary case came in 1957, a year after the famous "jam pots" were dropped, an AMC gearbox replaced the Burman four-speeder and a 600cc version developed such a nasty habit of breaking the crankshaft that the makers were forced to spend some of their hard-earned income on expensive Nodular material.

All this happened at a time when AMC, embracing AJS, Matchless, Norton, James and Francis Barnett, had splashed one million pounds — a lot of money in those days — on re-tooling their old fashioned Plumstead plant.

With slightly different bumps on timing case covers, to distinguish them, the original 500 Springtwins had 66x72mm bore and stroke dimensions.

This grew to a 600, with 72x72mm square motor and eventually a 650 stroked to 79mm, which came out in 1959.

The design formed the basis of the G45 500 racing twin with finned rocker box covers. And although Donald Heather, then managing director, was notoriously reluctant to lend his bikes for press road tests, one privileged scribe rode a CSR 600 sports to MIRA, near Nuneaton, and did 100 miles in one hour.

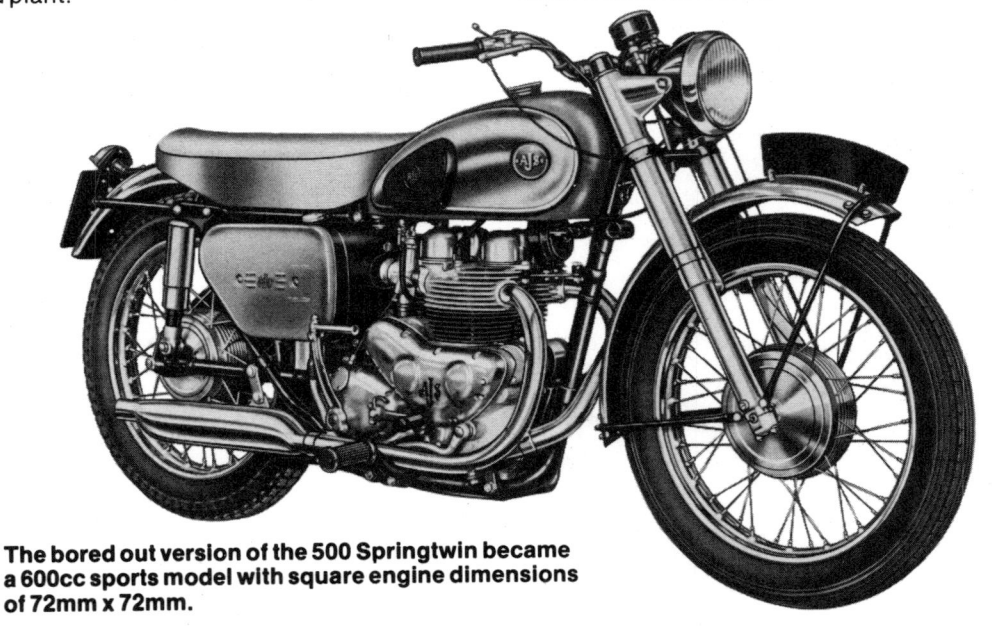

The bored out version of the 500 Springtwin became a 600cc sports model with square engine dimensions of 72mm x 72mm.

Specification — AJS 500 Springtwin

ENGINE: Air cooled, twin cylinder, overhead valve four-stroke. Bore and stroke 66mm x 72mm. Capacity 498cc. Compression ratio 7 or 8 to 1. Single Amal carburettor.

TRANSMISSION: Primary drive by chain, rear drive by chain. Multi-plate clutch in oil bath. Four-speed foot change Burman gearbox. Overall ratios 13.9, 8.9, 6.9 and 5.3 to 1.

ELECTRICAL: 6 volt, 13 amp hour battery charged by Lucas dynamo. Separate magneto with manual advance and retard. Seven-inch head-lamp with twin sidelights.

EQUIPMENT: Kickstarter, twinseat, central and prop stands.

CAPACITIES: 3½ gallon petrol tank, 4 pint oil tank.

WHEELS: Steel rims. Quickly detachable rear wheel with pull out spindle. 3.25 x 19in. front tyre, 3.50 x 19in. rear.

BRAKES: 7in. drum brakes front and rear. Full width alloy hubs with straight pull spokes.

SUSPENSION: Teledraulic front fork, swinging arm rear suspension with AMC shock absorbers.

DIMENSIONS: Seat height 30½in, wheelbase 55¼in, ground clearance 5½in, overall length 86¼in, weight 394lbs.

MANUFACTURERS: Associated Motor Cycles Ltd, Plumstead Road, Woolwich, London SE5.

OWNER'S STORY

72 touring miles a gallon

A TT fan for over 25 years, Eddy Powell, a painter and decorator from Shrewsbury, Salop, paid just £30 for his pristine condition 1955 AJS Springtwin in 1963. It is probably worth ten times as much today.

"I was only the third owner. I had the original log book until the "Swansea" changeover. The first owner lived in Yorkshire and I bought it from a Wellington garage where it has been part exchanged."

Mr Powell recalls owning a Matchless Springtwin of the same period: 'I had a G9 which cost £200 plus £40 purchase tax in 1955. I changed the oil regularly and did 60,000 miles on the original bottom end.

"The AJS is on its second speedo so I cannot be sure of the mileage. I don't ride it much nowadays: only in the summer. I have never had more than 90mph on the clock but it will easily better 70 miles to the gallon. The distance from my home to the Liverpool docks is 72 miles and a gallon gets me there without being drained out if I stick to touring speeds.

"A vibration period between 60-65 mph is never more than a tingle and disappears when you go quicker. Passengers feel it more through the pillion footrests than the rider. Seating is original and is still comfortable by modern standards but the suspension is a bit too soft if you gun it.

"I find the brakes adequate but I was spoilt by the super stoppers of the DBD34 Gold Star I had before buying the Springtwin.

"The old silencers rotted so I replaced them with a pattern close to the correct shape. The bags of my Britax panniers are a bit faded but they were available as optional extras on AMC bikes of the period.

"An oil leak on the dynamo at the front is the only smear and it just needs a new cork gasket."

WD Ariel 350

Of the several makes of motor cycles used by the armed forces and civilian services during and after World War II, the 350cc single cylinder ohv Ariel was by far the most popular with the Don-Rs.

Derived from the famed line of sporting Red Hunter models — which found their greatest success during the 60s with Sammy Miller's legendary 500cc trials bike, the 1940s WD model was in fact based on the 1939 ISDT works machines.

Specification — WD Ariel 350

ENGINE: Air cooled, single cylinder, overhead valve four-stroke. Cast iron barrel and head. Bore and stroke 72mm x 85mm. Capacity 347cc. Compression ratio 7.4 to 1. Amal carburettor.

TRANSMISSION: Single roller primary and secondary chains. Multi-plate clutch in oil. Engine shaft shock absorber. Four-speed foot-change gearbox. Overall ratios: 15.2, 9.72, 7.5 and 5.72 to 1.

ELECTRICAL: Lucas 56 watt Magdyno ignition with manual advance and retard, 6 volt, 12 amp hour battery, voltage control box, 7in. headlamp.

EQUIPMENT: Kickstarter, spring saddle, twin tool boxes, panniers, field prop stand, rear stand, forged footrests.

CAPACITIES: 2½ gallon petrol tank, 5 pint oil tank.

WHEELS: Steel rims, cast iron hubs, 3.25 x 19in. tyres front and rear.

BRAKES: 7in. drums front and rear. Fulcrum adjusters.

SUSPENSION: Girder front fork with central compression spring and lateral extension springs. Rigid back end.

DIMENSIONS: Seat height 28½in, ground clearance 5½in, wheelbase 55in, overall length 86in, weight 332lbs.

MANUFACTURERS: Ariel Motors Ltd, Selly Oak, Birmingham 29.

From scrap to a showpiece. Much of this 1941 WD Ariel 350 was found lying in a ditch. It took over two years to collect the rest.

Indeed, one might describe the WNH military model as the world's first trial bike; for unlike the military machines of other manufacturers, whose WD models were essentially standard roadsters, the Ariel was designed for cross-country riding and featured a two-inch longer front fork than standard to provide increased ground clearance.

The single cylinder Ariel, designed as a 500 in 1934, was popular with clubmen for the intentional ease with which it could be converted for trials, scrambles and grass track racing where it achieved considerable success from the efforts of L. W. E. Hartley, whose bikes were raced by such riders as Jock West, Peter Ferbrache and Harry Ditchburn, Barry Ditchburn's father. Bill Boddice also started his racing career on an Ariel.

With the bottom half of the engine unchanged, the cylinder head was redesigned in 1938 by the total enclosure of the overhead valve gear. At this same time, 250 and 350cc versions were introduced.

Needless to say, by utilising 500cc components, these smaller editions were relatively heavy. The 350 weighed about the same weight (350lbs) which, with some 19bhp, scarcely provided dragster performance. However, with low gearing, the WD models were nippy — capable of about 70mph — extremely reliable and economical on fuel.

Some 43,000 of these machines were produced for the war effort and continued in service for some 20 years after the war. However, as these became redundant, they were sold off and lucky lads were buying a new model in 1946 for just £70.

Right: The 350cc Ariel motors produced only 19bhp, but were very nippy with low gearing.
Above: Complete with headlamp mask, Ted Cotton's WD Ariel is astonishingly authentic. And how about that for a prop stand!

OWNER'S STORY

Probably the best bikes in the service

Motor cycles didn't interest Ted Cotton, of Northampton, until he was 'ordered' to become interested while serving with the Army in North Africa in 1944.

"Motor cycles meant nothing to me", he recalls. "I was an auto-electrician by trade, but trades meant nothing in the Army. It's rank that counts and as a corporal I happened to be about when the corporal in charge of our motor cycle section got knocked out. 'Right', said the Captain, 'Corporal Cotton do you know anything about motor cycles?' 'No Sir', I replied. 'Well, you will', he told me. 'You are in charge of the motor cycle section.'

"The bikes in our unit (Royal Army Service Corps) were 350cc Ariels and they were probably the best bikes in the service.

"One of those was the first bike I ever rode — and being in charge of the section, I had to show that I could ride a motor cycle! My mechanics were two Egyptians and two German prisoners of war — and those two knew more about motor bikes than I ever will. One of them worked for BMW before the war. I have often wondered what became of them.

"Somehow I managed it, without falling off. From that moment motor cycles became part of my life.

"For a good many years after the war they were just a hobby; I was always tinkering around with them. As an electrician, I worked for the Post Office for nine years, but in 1955 I decided to open a small motor cycle business of my own."

With a small showroom and workshop in a Northampton back-street, Ted's main living is with repairs. The fact that he can do a good job is clearly reflected in the gleamingly restored ex-WD 350 Ariel built from a rusting heap of bits and pieces.

An active member of the Vintage Club, Ted also has an immaculate, original condition, 1927 model M 250cc Levis and a 1927 AJS 1000cc vee-twin, along with a home-built featherbed Norton combo fitted with a 650 Triumph twin engine. "They keep me busy" he continued, "but I got inspired by a Vintage Club friend of mine who restored a WD Matchless so I thought I'd find one. But it had to be an Ariel, just the same as the first bike I ever rode in the Army.

"That was in 1972. A customer told me of an army Ariel lying in a field on a farm, but what a mess! It was a heap of rust lying in a ditch. All that remained was the bare frame, front fork and wheels, headlamp shell and rear mudguard — but they were genuine bits.

"I bought these and then started to scratch around for the rest. I decided to leave the work until I had got all the bits to assemble a complete bike — and this took me over two years. The one good stroke of luck was that I found a complete engine which, like the frame, was made in 1941. The Burman gearbox had to be made up from spares, as was just about everything else. The pannier bags came from Belgium; I swapped a headlamp mask for them!

"The prop stand I found in somebody's garden. They were using it as a potato dibber. I found the spring-clip to hold the prop stand on a stall at an auto jumble, where it had been in a box for three years. The fellow who sold it to me didn't know what it was."

With the reconstruction of his bike, Ted has gone to great lengths to ensure that all possible parts he has used are genuine WD components, even though standard Ariel spares are interchangeable. On this point he admits to one particular variation. He has fitted the better quality steel flywheels from a Red Hunter in place of the cast iron originals. Similarly, a modern, miniature Japanese battery is concealed inside the old unit.

The authenticity of this machine is quite astonishing, even to the detail in the RASC unit insignia flashes painted on the petrol tank. "I had a sign writer do them from my old shoulder flash". The condition of this bike is such that it has won a concours d'elegance in an international motor cycle rally where it stood against brand new condition modern machines.

The one feature which takes it away, just a trifle from the war years is that its olive green paintwork shines brilliantly from his constant attention. "During the war, they were kept dull so as not to cause a reflection that may be seen by the enemy. We even painted the engines in the desert and flung sand on wet paint to help the camouflage. But I couldn't do that to this bike."

Ariel VB

The simplicity and slogging power of its old fashioned side valve engine made the 600 Ariel VB a firm favourite with family sidecarrists before the advent of the Mini.

One of the last examples of a breed which came into its own in hilly country with mum and dad on the pillion and the kids and luggage and perhaps granny in the chair, the VB was pensioned off in 1958.

It had been around for as long as most people who rode bikes, because they were cheaper than cars, could remember. For although the last of the line was cosmetically modernised, its engine went back to 1931.

Ariel already had a 500cc side valve single when the Kaiser war broke out, in 1914, but the VB was actually a development of the single lungers Val

Left: Ariel VB — last side valve machine to be made by the company. Above: With alloy head and cast iron barrel, the engine was prone to overheating.

Page designed in 1926. The original cylinder bore of 86.4mm remained unaltered, but the stroke was twice increased to give a greater engine capacity. The 102mm stroke was introduced in 1936, giving an actual capacity of 598cc.

Earlier VBs had 550cc engines, but there were other landmarks in the evolution of these hard-working flat heads. In 1932, when Edward Turner was responsible for the Red Hunters, the VB received a new seven stud cast iron head. The iron head was replaced by a nine stud alloy head in 1951, when valve size was increased, and the compression ratio was raised to a dizzy 6 to 1 in 1955. An air cleaner was part of post-war modernisation.

Cycle parts underwent inevitable fashion changes. While most pre-war VBs had rigid back ends, plunger rear suspension was available in 1939. It was designed by Frank Anstey, best remembered for redesigning the valve gear of ohv models during his four years with Ariel.

The great virtue of the VB was its solid design and great pulling power. Even in the 1930s, it looked dated compared with the 600cc overhead camshaft square four which was replaced by the pushrod Squariel.

The combination of a long stroke and a fairly high kick starter ratio required a definite knack on cold mornings. And as the exhaust note was never remarkable for its quietness, the hallmark of a good neighbour was his methodical starting drill.

OWNER'S STORY

Nothing much to go wrong with it

Ariel owner Norman Hartley, from Kirkby-in-Ashfield, Notts, paid only £10 for the collection of bits from which he rebuilt his 1956 VB.

His first machine was a second-hand 1950 Ariel Red Hunter with a plunger frame. The Ariel bug had bitten him, and his next bike was a brand new Huntmaster. Later, he bought a used 1952 Square Four which he exchanged in 1959 for a brand new Ariel Leader.

Marriage and a family meant leaving motor cycling for a time, but the bug was still with him and he wanted to get back to motor cycling with a British bike. When Mr Harley found bits and pieces

Routine was to set the ignition lever at the three-quarter advance position, shut the air lever, dab the carburettor tickler without waiting for the bowl to flood, then ease the piston over compression by using the exhaust valve lifter.

An almighty swing on the kick starter and a shade of throttle would generally produce a first kick getaway. And while retarding the ignition would cure a tendency for the engine to pink when pulling hard, the exhaust note was distinctly loud.

The VB would cruise indefinitely at 40 to 45mph but top speed with a child-adult chair was under 60mph. The long stroke engine was economical, giving around 60mpg at 40mph, but it always had a nasty habit of overheating.

The alloy head helped, but it took only a few miles for the beast to become hot enough to boil a kettle. Overheating exhaust valves led to distortion, burned valves or blown gaskets. A successful modification was to fit a 500cc Red Hunter valve guide and turned down valve.

Incredibly, VBs were actually raced in the early days when careful tuning gave a top speed of about 95mph at Brooklands. Many years later, Mike Hailwood failed to blow up a VB hitched to a float for delivering motor cycles during a youthful escapade from his father's bike shop in Oxford.

While most VBs formed the better half of family outfits, a number of engines were used for motor trikes in the 1950s when a new specimen, with its characteristic square tappet cover on the side of the engine, cost the princely sum of £186 including purchase tax!

---

of an Ariel VB — the frame, log book, engine and wheels, he bought these for about £10.

"I seemed to travel thousands of miles chasing around for bits," he recalled. "I was looking for photographs and information as well. The bike is now as standard as I can get it, going from the photos. The colours are not standard."

A specialist in old British bikes, Tony Cooper of Birmingham, supplied a new dual seat, front mudguard, silencer and control cables. The repainting and rebuilding took 18 months.

"The bike is used every day, so I did not want to lay out a lot of money to put it in concours condition. I joined the Ariel club because I don't think you can afford not to be in the club if you are rebuilding a bike."

The Ariel's wheels were re-spoked with new rims, and a new exhaust pipe was purchased through the Ariel Owners Club. Mr. Harley undertook the repainting task, and first had to strip about a quarter of an inch of paint away from the frame. He repainted in enamel.

All that is left to do on this machine is to replace some second-hand parts with new ones. The engine is still on its standard bore and piston, but some bearings and bushes were replaced along with valve guides and springs.

Even on solo gearing (Mr Harley bought the bits in sidecar specification) the side valve engine does not rev beyond 4,400rpm, but with its long stroke (86 x 102mm bore and stroke) provides enough power for cruising comfortably at 55 to 60mph. The bike returns over 70mpg.

Electricity is generated by magneto and dynamo, and the lighting is six volt.

Mr Harley says the swinging arm frame gives a comfortable ride. "What I like about it is that it is simple and there is nothing much to go wrong with it. It has enough power and speed and should be reliable. I am looking forward to many thousands of miles of trouble-free riding."

Specification — Ariel VB

ENGINE: Air cooled, single cylinder, side valve four-stroke. Bore and stroke 86.4mm x 102mm. Capacity 598cc. Compression ratio 6 to 1. Cast iron barrel. Alloy head. Three-bearing crankshaft. Amal carburettor.

TRANSMISSION: Single row primary and secondary chains. Multi-plate clutch with cork inserts in separate compartment. Burman four-speed footchange gearbox. Overall ratios 15.15, 9.72, 7.5 and 5.72 to 1.

ELECTRICAL: Lucas Magdyno with manual ignition control. 7in. headlamp.

EQUIPMENT: Kickstart, dualseat, roll-on centre stand, detachable air filter, steering damper.

CAPACITIES: 4½ gallon petrol tank, 6 pint oil tank.

WHEELS: Steel rims, cast iron hubs, 3.25 x 19in. tyres front and rear.

BRAKES: 7in. diameter drum brakes front and rear. Fulcrum adjusters.

SUSPENSION: Telescopic front fork with hydraulic damping. Box section swinging arm and hydraulic shockers at rear.

DIMENSIONS: Seat height 31in, ground clearance 5½in, wheelbase 56in, overall length 86in, weight 370lbs.

MANUFACTURERS: Ariel Motors Ltd, Selly Oak, Birmingham 29.

Ariel Huntmaster

The Ariel Huntmaster was the third British six-fifty vertical twin to appear after the war. It came out in 1954 and proved a worthy companion to the BSA and Triumph models already on the market.

Bridging the gap between the 500 Ariel Red Hunter single and the 1000 Ariel Square Four, it was in fact a cleverly disguised 650 BSA Golden Flash with an engine made at the parent BSA factory.

The best change was probably the provision of an inspection cap in the rocker box cover to visibly check the location of pushrods when replacing them.

With different crankcase castings, primary case, and Burman gearbox to distinguish it from the basic A10, the FH 650 remained in production until 1958 when the Selly Oak, Birmingham, factory, switched its efforts to the famous 250 Ariel Leader two stroke twin.

While the 646cc (70 x 84mm) iron engine, along with the front fork, were from BSA, Ariel engineers came up with a new duplex frame with box section swinging arm for the rear suspension.

Developing about 35bhp at 5,600 rpm, the Huntmaster was a sturdy roadster with steering geometry suitable for either solo or sidecar work. The low compression engine (6.5 to 1) was so flexible that many charioteers didn't bother to change sprockets.

Originally catalogued at £230.40, including British purchase tax, the Ariel was good for nearly 100mph in solo trim and about 70mph when harnessed to a chair. In both cases, petrol consumption was seldom under 50mpg.

Clive Bennett, a former development engineer who took part in a sidecar demo with Bob Ray and George Buck during which they visited seven countries in seven days, recalls testing a prototype at 112mph and clocking 132mph downwind with a tuned engine at the MIRA test track.

Early models had plain headlamps and single sided brakes. These were later replaced by very nice alloy full width brakes, and a distinctive headlamp cowling.

Tan or black leathercloth dualseat covering was optional. And while maroon paintwork was the most popular, export black with bright orange mudguards was readily available from 1957 onwards. Chromed flutes, originally plated on the tank, became detachable in 1956, but this distinctive feature, reminiscent of flutes on the bonnets of Vauxhall cars,

Based on the BSA A10, Ariel's Huntmaster FH650 was a nicely proportioned roadster with more than a hint of quality.

Specification — Ariel Huntmaster

ENGINE: Air cooled, twin cylinder, overhead valve four-stroke. Cast iron barrel and head. Light alloy con rods. Plain big ends. Bore and stroke 70mm x 84mm. Capacity 646cc. Compression ratio 6.5 to 1. Amal carburettor.

TRANSMISSION: Single roller primary and secondary chains. Multi-plate wet clutch in alloy case with inspection panel. Burman four-speed footchange gearbox. Overall ratios 11.55, 7.4, 5.7 and 4.35 to 1.

ELECTRICAL: Lucas magneto with auto advance. Separate 56 watt Lucas dynamo with output controlled by CVC unit. 7in. headlamp.

EQUIPMENT: Detachable aircleaner, roll-on centre stand, front stand, kickstarter, pillion footrests, dualseat, headlamp casquette, steering damper. Rear chain case extra. Sidecar gearing and suspensions available.

CAPACITIES: 4 gallon petrol tank, 6 pint oil tank.

WHEELS: Steel rims, full width alloy hubs front and rear.

OWNER'S STORY

BRAKES: 7in drums front and rear. Fulcrum adjusters. Linkage from left to right for rear brake cable.

SUSPENSION: Telescopic front fork, box section rear swinging arm with Armstrong shockers.

DIMENSIONS: Seat height 31in, ground clearance 5½in, overall length 86½in, weight 365lbs.

MANUFACTURERS: Ariel Motors Ltd, Selly Oak, Birmingham 29.

The odd quirk at high speed but very stable

A Northampton signwriter who deplores the demise of the British bike industry, Gordon Hamilton-Grey bought his 1957 Ariel Huntmaster secondhand in 1960 and still rides it every day.

"I paid £135 for it, at a time when a new BMW cost £340, and the only time it has let me down was when a chain link dropped out after 30,000 miles" said Mr Hamilton-Grey.

Although he had the wheels rebuilt, the crankshaft reground, and the cylinders rebored at 40,000 miles, he retains the original magneto and the chrome of his filler cap has been rubbed down to the brass.

"I rode it as a sidecar combo for ten years. It would do about 80 on the clock four up with a chair. I've never had more than 100 on the clock in solo trim but the vibration was pretty horrific.

"Apart from the odd quirk on corners at high speed, the bike is very stable. It is not particularly quick but the brakes have always got me out of trouble and the six-volt lights are quite adequate."

His only previous mount was a 98cc New Hudson autocycle. He chose the Huntmaster because he liked the look of it. He even passed his test on it back in 1961. "One day I'll get around to restoring it to concours finish," he says.

was eventually dropped and '57, '58 and early '59 versions sported a non-fluted tank held by a single bolt with a chromed strap.

Because the final drive was on the left, a linkage was used to transfer motion of the left-sided brake pedal to the other side. A rear chaincase was available on later models but, with such useful features as a separate cover on the primary case to reach the clutch, solid engineering coupled with tractable and lively top gear performance were the Huntmaster's greatest assets. It weighed about 430lbs.

Good for nearly 100mph, the iron engine developed 35bhp at 5,600rpm. A low compression ratio gave it great flexibility.

Ariel Square Four

Last of Britain's 1000cc superbikes, the Ariel Square Four was never a real road burner but a smooth and docile flagship with a performance far superior to most cars of its era.

While the 4G Mark II was good for over 90mph, and could sometimes top the magic ton before it ran out of breath, its most endearing characteristic was the pulling power and flexibility of its engine.

Affectionately known as the Squariel because of the square formation of its four cylinders, the 997cc machine (65mm x 75mm bore and stroke) packed so much torque that it could actually be started in top gear without unduly stressing the clutch.

As a solo, the Squariel would pull top gear from 10 mph to maximum. Its phenomenal torque range had to be believed. Not surprisingly, it became a firm favourite with the family sidecar fraternity.

Originally designed by Edward Turner, later famous as creator of the Triumph twins and Daimler V8 engines, the Square Four began in the early 1930s as a 500 and subsequently 600cc sports job with chain driven overhead camshaft and forward facing carburettor.

The first 1000cc version was introduced in 1937. It was extensively redesigned, with pushrods for the valve gear of a cast iron cylinder block and head which remained in production with minor changes until after World War II. Claimed power output of the 4G Mark I was 38 bhp at 5,500 rpm.

While overheating of the rear cylinders was reduced by the adoption of an alloy head, with side manifolds similar to those of the old iron engine, inadequate cooling remained a problem even after the alloy-engined Mark II came along in 1954.

Watercooling would probably have solved this weakness but ingeniously coupled crankshafts presented another problem. The arrangement gave a power impulse every 180 degrees of engine rotation. Balancing was virtually perfect but the straight-cut coupling gears could be as noisy as the teeth of an old fashioned mangle. Worn couplings were more than audible when throttling downhill.

By raising compression to 7.2 to 1 when better petrol became available, the output of the Mark II was increased to 42bhp at 5,800rpm. Pre-ignition of the back cylinders, common on earlier models, was minimised on later models with SU carburettor instead of the original bi-starter Solex.

Other important changes included car type ignition, with a key switch under the dualseat, and a special

Beautiful Squariel restoration. Note the extra large oil tank and swinging link and plunger rear suspension.

Lucas 70 watt dynamo to charge a massive 20 amp battery made only for the Squariel.

A sleek headlamp cowl, along with a full width alloy front brake and an extra large oil tank, containing a full gallon of lubricant, readily distinguished the 1956 models from their predecessors.

Always on the heavy side, even after the alloy engine chopped 33lb off its overall weight, the Squariel tipped the scales at around 480lbs when Frank Anstey, a member of the Ariel design team, produced one of the most interesting innovations of the 1939 London motor cycle show.

While rival factories toyed with plunger back ends, Ariel sprang a swinging link system as unique as their big engine. It was not a complete solution to road-holding problems but, although the machines continued to be a bit of a handful at speed, the rear suspension worked well.

The ultimate version of this prestige bike never went into production.

Along with all Ariel four strokes, the Square Four, sometimes known as the Four Square by people who confused it with a brand of pipe tobacco, was shelved to make way for the Ariel Leader in 1958.

OWNER'S STORY
Easy motor that pulls like a Shirehorse

A rally enthusiast with the Welland Valley Sidecar Club, John Cooper became a Squariel owner almost by accident.

"I was looking for a new bike to pull a chair. I'd seen a Ural but there was a delivery delay. A test ride on the Ariel at a rally near Swindon impressed me with its pulling power.

"I'm a British bike fan really. And at £380, it was about the same price as the Russian twin" recalls Mr Cooper, a sheet metal training instructor from Bulkington, near Coventry.

His Square Four is a 1957 Mark II. It had been carefully maintained by its previous owners and had done considerable mileage as a sidecar hauler.

Back in solo trim, Mr Cooper's maroon Squariel awaited a bidder. "I've also got a couple of Velos. I'm thinking of getting a sports sidecar for the 500 Venom. I'll keep the 350 Viper as a solo.

"The Squariel was mainly a summer bike. I hitched it to a Canterbury double adult for rallies with my wife and three children. Now they're growing, the eldest don't always want to come.

"The bike has always been on solo gearing, with a 25-tooth engine sprocket. We rarely go further than 150 miles from home but the recommended 22-tooth sprocket would be necessary in the Lake District.

"In 5,000 miles, the only major job I've undertaken is fitting new valves and springs. The springs are the same as an Austin A30. The engine is one of the easiest I have ever worked on.

"During the 50mph restrictions, petrol consumption averaged 44mpg. The outfit easily cruises at the legal limit.

"It is also a fabulous solo. Two-up, it will waffle from 30 to 95 in top gear. Top speed is about 105 mph. I've not ridden anything else quite like it. It is not a revvy motor like a Japanese four but pulls like a Shire horse.

"Because of the bike's 425lb, the brakes are not quite up to today's traffic conditions. Modern machines of a similar weight have double discs," concluded Mr Cooper, who made new silencers and a sheet metal imitation of the original battery.

An impressive looking engine offered a performance far superior to most cars of the day. The torque was phenomenal and Square Fours could be started in top gear.

Specification — Ariel Square Four

ENGINE: Air cooled, four cylinder, overhead valve four-stroke. Bore and stroke 65mm x 75mm. Capacity 997cc. Aluminium cylinder block with steel liners. Alloy head. Twin crankshafts on roller and plain bearings. Alloy con rods. Plain big ends. Compression ratio 7.2 to 1. SU variable choke carburettor.

TRANSMISSION: Geared crankshafts. Single roller primary and secondary chains. Three plate dry clutch. Engine sprocket shock absorber. Four-speed footchange gearbox. Overall ratios: 11.55, 7.40, 5.70 and 4.36 to 1.

ELECTRICAL: Lucas coil ignition with 70 watt dynamo, 20 amp hour battery, distributor and automatic advance and retard. 7½in. headlamp.

EQUIPMENT: Kickstarter, air cleaner, prop stand, rear stand, steering lock, steering damper.

CAPACITIES: 5 gallon petrol tank, 8 pint oil tank.

WHEELS: Steel rims, quickly detachable rear spindle. Full width alloy front hub. Cast iron single sided rear hub.

BRAKES: 8in. diameter drums front and rear. Car-type fulcrum adjusters.

SUSPENSIONS: Telescopic front fork, hydraulically damped. Trailing link and plunger rear suspension.

DIMENSIONS: Seat height 31in, ground clearance 5½in, overall length 86in, weight 480lbs.

MANUFACTURERS: Ariel Motors Ltd, Selly Oak, Birmingham 29.

Ariel Leader

First bike to win Motor Cycle News' Machine of the Year popularity poll, the 250 Ariel Leader was a refreshingly different twin-cylinder two stroke with pressed steel bodywork instead of a conventional tubular frame.

Although rather vulnerable in accidents, it was a truly all purpose machine in which snazzy styling and effective weather protection went hand in hand with exceptional road holding and enough power to live with modern traffic.

Launched in summer 1958 after three years of development, it was the brainchild of Ariel supremo Ken Whistance and chief designer Val Page who, many years before, was responsible for the best selling singles from the Selly Oak, Birmingham, factory.

The Leader was ahead of its time in many ways. It was almost revolutionary. But the British power unit was of German descent, being based on a pre-war Adler which conveniently went out of production in 1957. Nowadays better known for typewriters, Adler made bikes from the turn of the century.

Biggest difference was the method of joining the two halves of the 180 degree three-bearing crankshaft. Each half had its own full flywheels and could be removed without taking the engine out.

Instead of the expensive gear coupling on the Frankfurt-built Adler, Ariel cut costs with a bolt and taper connection, a captive bolt and hollow spindle being used to split the shaft.

The 249cc (54mm x 54mm bore and stroke) power pack incorporated a Burman four-speed box from which the clusters could also be removed with the engine in situ. The clutch featured a transmission shock absorber and rattle-proof corrugated plates and body.

Designed with enclosure in mind, the Ariel unit was more functional than pretty. It had inclined cylinders with horizontal fins, breathed through a single Amal Monobloc and got its sparks from a normal Lucas alternator and contact breaker.

The engine was suspended from the extensions of a box-section beam frame hidden under the body panels. Presswork was contracted out to Homers, the Midland motor cycle tank specialists.

While the 2½ gallon petrol tank was slotted inside the box frame, with a filler cap under the seat, the main body pressing bulged into a tank-shaped parcel compartment with lockable lid. Spacious enough for a pre-space helmet, the compartment hid a toggle for the seat and a steering lock.

A sensation in 1958, the Ariel Leader was probably the most successful all-weather bike ever produced.

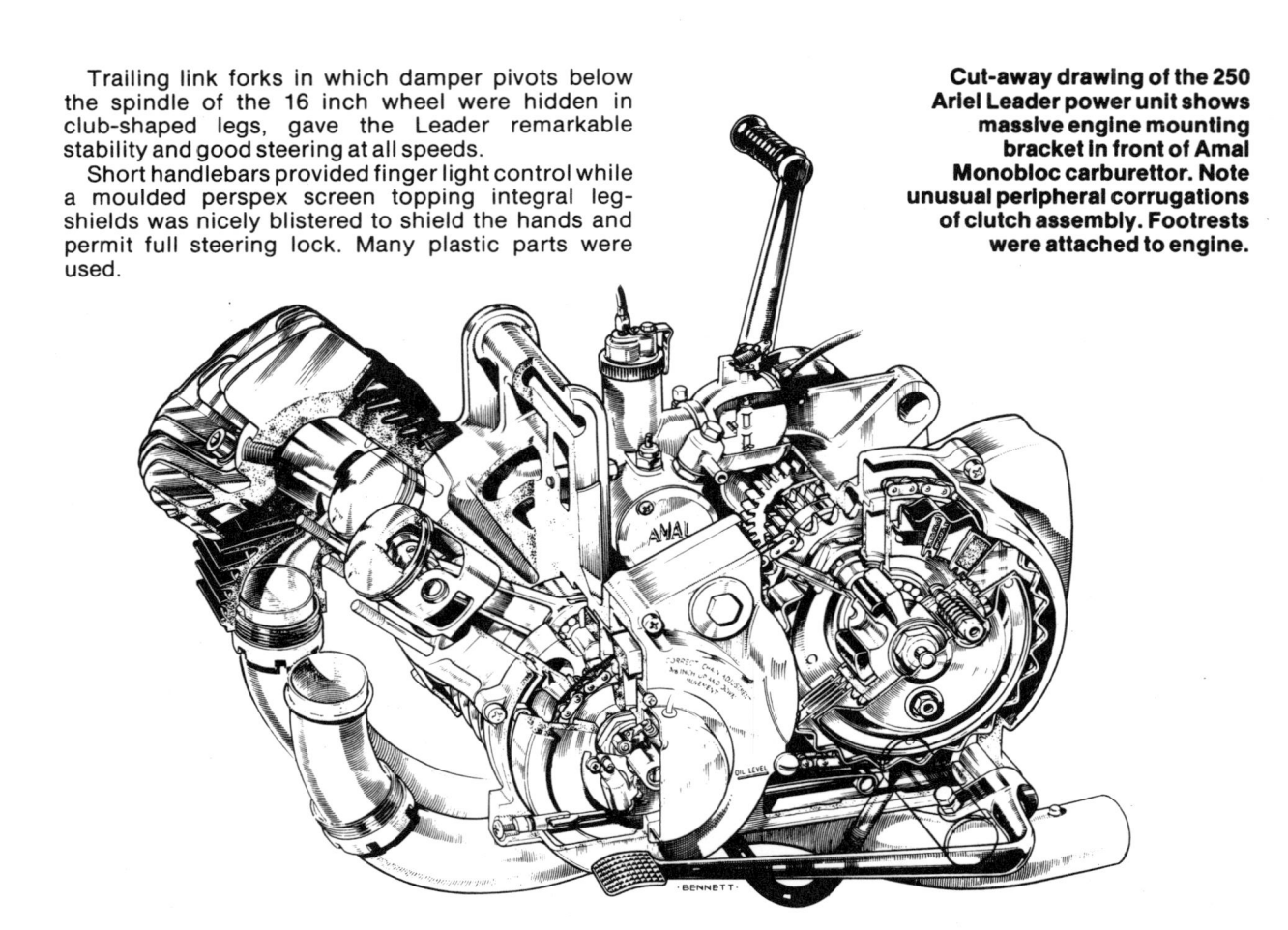

Trailing link forks in which damper pivots below the spindle of the 16 inch wheel were hidden in club-shaped legs, gave the Leader remarkable stability and good steering at all speeds.

Short handlebars provided finger light control while a moulded perspex screen topping integral legshields was nicely blistered to shield the hands and permit full steering lock. Many plastic parts were used.

Cut-away drawing of the 250 Ariel Leader power unit shows massive engine mounting bracket in front of Amal Monobloc carburettor. Note unusual peripheral corrugations of clutch assembly. Footrests were attached to engine.

Specification — Ariel Leader

ENGINE: Air cooled, twin cylinder two-stroke. Bore and stroke 54mm x 54mm. Capacity 249cc. Compression ratio 8.25 to 1. Single Amal Monobloc carburettor.

TRANSMISSION: Primary drive by chain, rear drive by chain. Multi-plate clutch in oil. Four-speed footchange gearbox. Overall ratios 19.0, 11.0, 7.8 and 5.9 to 1.

ELECTRICAL: 6 volt, 13 amp hour battery charged by Lucas 50 watt alternator. Coil ignition with fixed timing. Pre-focus 6in. headlamp.

EQUIPMENT: Kickstarter, luggage compartment in dummy tank, leg shields and windscreen. Other accessories extra.

CAPACITIES: 2½ gallon petroil (25 to 1) tank under seat.

WHEELS: Steel rims, cast alloy hubs, 3.25 x 16in. tyres front and rear.

BRAKES: 6in. full width front and rear. Fulcrum adjusters.

SUSPENSION: Trailing link front fork, swinging arm rear fork, Amstrong hydraulic shockers front and rear.

DIMENSIONS: Seat height 31in, wheelbase 51in, ground clearance 5in, weight 330lbs with all extras.

MANUFACTURERS: Ariel Motors Ltd, Selly Oak, Birmingham 29.

Refinements like a retractable lifting handle, a plastic toggle for the choke, a stop light operated by both brakes, and a small dashboard lever to adjust the headlamp beam reflected remarkable attention to detail.

Twin exhausts usually emitted distinctive smoke trails but an induction silencer helped to lower the noise level so successfully that only the drumming of the panels and the squeaking of the suspensions could be heard in the saddle.

Weighing 300lb without extras the basic Leader cost £209 11s 7d. Top speed was around 70mph and fuel consumption in the region of 60 mpg.

Whitewall tyres were an extra luxury but Leader owners could gild the lily with a galaxy of specially designed accessories, including matching panniers with locking lids and detachable holdalls, a cast aluminium rear carrier, winkers, prop stand, two-way parking light for the dash board, eight-day clock, inspection light and ignition timer, a telescopic jack, and a chromed rear bumper.

Although Ariel stepped up production to 250 a week after discontinuing their range of four strokes, the Leader was not everybody's cup of tea. Something like 20,000 were built before the Ariel management decided to strip the Leader down to its bikini and sprang the equally successful Arrow and subsequent Golden Arrow.

OWNER'S STORY

The range of accessories was fascinating

After a crash in which the box frame was damaged, the 1960 Leader with which George Browning won the concours d'elegance at a national Ariel owners rally, stood at the bottom of a garden for ten years.

"I bought the wreck to have a spare engine for my Ariel Arrow. Then I obtained another frame and decided to rebuild the machine with all the accessories," said Mr Browning, an aero design engineer from Cambridge.

"I was fascinated by the array of accessories available for the Leader. I have now got most of them but have so far failed to locate an inspection light cum ignition gadget which plugged into a socket under the bars.

"Some of the goodies took a lot of finding. The most elusive was the Smiths eight-day clock. I had previously fitted an electric clock. Then I stumbled on the genuine article while sniffing round a friend's workshop.

"I spent many hours rubbing down rusty components before I had them stove enamelled in black and white, the finish favoured by police forces who used Ariel Leaders for patrol duties. The whole thing cost me about £120.

"The perspex screen is original. It survived the accident which distorted the steering head but a small corner was broken off. Rubber mouldings specially made for the Leader tend to perish and are quite hard to find.

"I got the Leader from Huntingdon, where I also bought my Arrow. I use the Arrow for green-laning and the Leader for commuting and a spot of touring. The more I use it the more I like it.

"It is remarkably reliable. I took the heads off after 10,000 miles. Apart from that, all I've done is fit a new set of points.

350 BSA B31

A rugged work horse which survived a chronic attack of middle-age spread, the evergreen BSA B31 of the mid-fifties was one of the heaviest 350s the British industry ever shelled out.

Tipping the scales at 30 stone (420lbs with extras and full tanks), the 1956 version of this bread-and-butter roadster was the victim of a policy of rationalisation which loaded it with a lot of dead weight.

No lightweight in its original rigid and plunger spring frame versions, the B31 started to put on weight at an alarming rate when it acquired a hefty duplex frame which it shared with BSA 500s and 650s.

Above: The 348cc overhead valve engine that powered B31s had a sporting ancestry going back to the 'thirties.
Left: Once a Home Office hack, this B31 has been transformed into a replica of the Earls Court exhibition models.

Always popular with utility riders because of its comparatively low running costs, it lost some of its appeal as more models came on the market, but approximately 8000 a year were manufactured by the Small Heath, Birmingham, factory, before it was pensioned off in favour of the lighter 350 B40 in 1960.

Powered by a 348cc (71 x 88mm bore and stroke) overhead valve engine with a sporting ancestry going back to the 'thirties, the B31 was converted to swinging arm rear suspension in 1954.

At the 1955 Earls Court Show, the B31 (£200 17s. 8d. with purchase tax) sported Ariel brakes which it retained for a couple of seasons. When Ariel four strokes were killed off, in 1958, the B31 was fitted with Triumph stoppers. This was all part of the rationalisation policy which standardised as many parts as possible within the BSA group.

Excellent when dry, Ariel's full width alloy brakes were not exactly watertight. The weakness was accentuated by a period during which Ferodo green linings were tried. Distinctly superior for normal braking, the green linings turned into blotting paper when wet and caused a few memorable moments!

Virtually identical to the B33 — the main difference being the bore of the 499cc engine (85 x 88mm) — the B31 was a really robust machine with a cast iron cylinder and head and fully enclosed overhead valve gear.

An alloy primary case similar to that of BSA twins was a big improvement over the earlier steel

Specification — 350 BSA B31

ENGINE: Air cooled, single cylinder, pushrod, overhead valve four stroke. Bore and stroke 71mm x 88mm. Capacity 348cc. Compression ratio 6.5 to 1. Cast iron cylinder and head. Roller big end. Dry sump lubrication. Amal Monobloc carburettor.

TRANSMISSION: Multi-plate clutch in oil. Single roller primary and rear chains. Four-speed footchange gearbox. Overall ratios: 14.42, 9.86, 6.77 and 5.58 to 1.

ELECTRICAL: Lucas magdyno ignition and lighting. Manual advance and retard control. 6 volt 12 amp hour battery charged through voltage control box. 7in headlamp.

CAPACITIES: 4 gallons petrol, 5½ pints oil.

EQUIPMENT: Kickstarter, steering damper, centre stand, dualseat, prop stand (extra), air cleaner.

WHEELS: Steel rims with full width alloy hubs. Tyres 3.25 x 19in front and 3.50 x 19in rear.

BRAKES: 7in diameter front and rear. Fulcrum adjusters.

SUSPENSION: BSA telescopic front fork and swinging arm rear suspension with oil damped shockers.

DIMENSIONS: Seat height 31½in, ground clearance 5½in, wheelbase 57in, overall length 86in, weight 420lbs.

MANUFACTURERS: BSA Motor Cycles Ltd, Armoury Road, Small Heath, Birmingham 11.

OWNER'S STORY
Wreck that became a show special

A former trials rider whose passion for bikes is still strong enough for him to jump on his 1000 BMW for a quick trip to Germany, Ray Reardon had several B31s when a BSA was his only form of transport.

A perfectionist who was a ship's joiner before he became an interior designer and shopfitter, he rebuilt a 1956 B31 from what was virtually a wreck into a glittering replica of the show models the BSA factory prepared for display on their stand at Earls Court.

"The special show finish was generally entrusted to BSA apprentices. It involved buffing and polishing alloy castings, chrome instead of cadmium plating, and better than standard paint work and finish.

"They brought out the quality of the machine. I have a pretty photographic memory and I always said that, one day, I would build one up in the same way," recalls Mr Reardon of Ongar, Essex, where he and his son have eight bikes, including two B31s.

"I restored the bike as an extension of my work. It was advertised in Motor Cycle News by a teenager who was the sixth owner after the Home Office auctioned the bike in 1970.

"It had 89,000 miles on the clock, the big-end was clapped out, the green paintwork had been touched up with black and red, the headlamp nacelle was squashed and battered, the exhaust pipe was flattened and grazed, the front mudguard was damaged, and there were 22 dents in the tank.

pressings while the 5½ pints oil tank and deeply valanced mudguards were common to bigger bikes in the range.

Although an air filter-cum-induction silencer stifled some of its power, performance of the slow-revving B31 motor was not unduly affected by the extra weight it carried.

Top speed was about the same as a 125 Honda but the B31 was probably more economical. While it took around 20 seconds to stagger over a standing quarter mile, and would just about do 73mph in top, it would cruise at 60-65mph on half throttle and average between 70 and 90 miles per gallon.

Thanks to the provision of an exhaust valve lifter to ease the piston over compression (only 6.5 to 1), and handlebar air and ignition controls, starting was almost invariably a first kick procedure.

For normal motoring, the ignition lever was best set on full advance but half-retard was handy for chuffing through city traffic or to ensure a good tickover.

With steering geometry similar to a sporting Gold Star, the B31 handled well. A prop stand was an extra. It reduced the ground clearance and tended to scrape the road on left handers but saved a lot of effort.

While the fully enclosed rear chain was another worthwhile extra which did not unduly affect the weight, a lifting handle was a must. For raising the B31 on its centre stand was no mean physical feat

"It took me about four months on and off to get the tank ready for chrome panelling. I got all the dents out, without using filler, and hunted for bits all over the country. The five sections of the rear chaincase all came from different places.

"I wanted to fit a spring washer under every nut and bolt so I made them ⅟₁₆th of an inch longer. Everything else is as original show finish, including genuine BSA transfers (there are three different types of pattern transfers on the market)."

BSA B40 SS90

If today a major motor cycle manufacturer was to introduce a new model of a well tried and tested mid range machine with its weight cut by a quarter and with a power increase — the effect would be shattering. Yet this is what BSA did when they introduced the B40 in 1960.

When BSA developed the 350cc B40 from the very successful 250cc C15 they created a machine which went on to dominate the off road competition world, and which in road going trim was a simple, reliable and economical mount.

To judge the significance of the step BSA took in bringing out this model compare it to the B31. The earlier model weighed a massive 420lb with extras and a full tank while the B40 weighed only 300lb.

Specification — BSA B40 SS90

ENGINE: Air cooled, single cylinder, pushrod, overhead valve four stroke. Bore and Stroke 79mm x 70mm. Capacity 343cc. Compression ratio 8.75 to 1. Iron barrel, alloy head. Amal Monobloc carburettor.

TRANSMISSION: Multi-plate clutch in oil. Duplex primary and secondary chains. Four-speed gearbox with footchange. Overall ratios 12.3, 9.6, 6.93 and 5.78 to 1.

ELECTRICAL: Distributor ignition, alternator, 6 volt 13 amp hour battery. 7in. headlamp.

CAPACITIES: 3 gallons petrol, 4 pints oil.

EQUIPMENT: Kickstarter, tool and battery cases, dual seat, prop and centre stands.

WHEELS: Steel rims carrying 3.25 x 18in. front tyre and 3.50 x 18in. rear.

BRAKES: 7in. single leading shoe front brake, 6in. rear.

SUSPENSION: Telescopic front forks, swinging arm rear.

DIMENSIONS: Seat height 32in, ground clearance 7in, wheelbase 54in, overall length 80in, weight 295lbs.

MANUFACTURER: BSA, Armoury Road, Birmingham 11.

Most eye-catching feature of the SS90 are chrome mudguards. Similarity with the C15 is apparent.

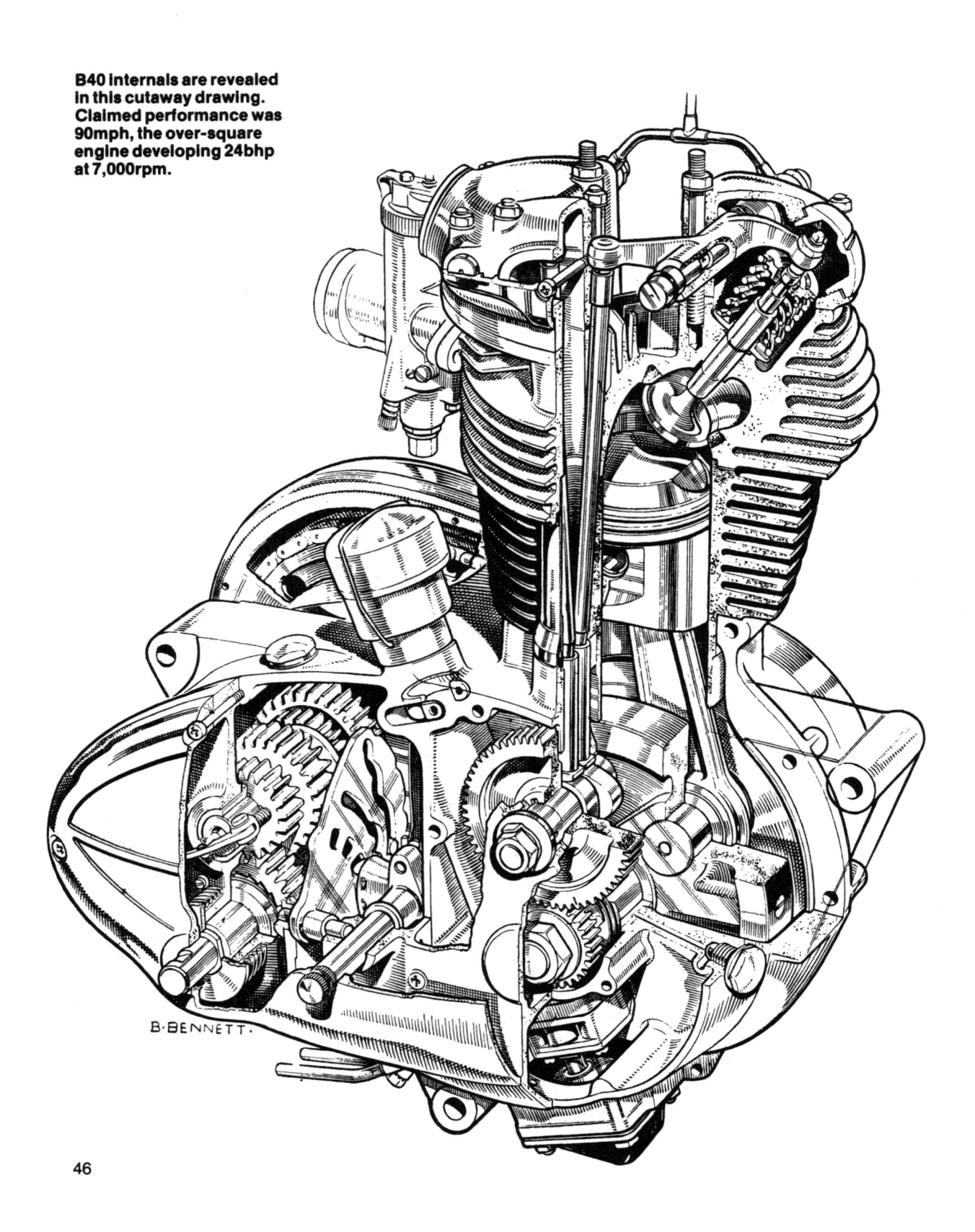

B40 internals are revealed in this cutaway drawing. Claimed performance was 90mph, the over-square engine developing 24bhp at 7,000rpm.

The top-line B40 was the SS90 model, claimed to have 90mph performance and an over-square engine developing 24bhp at 7,000rpm — quite a buzz-box in comparison to the slow revving B31.

The B40 was the brainchild of former BSA competitions manager Brian Martin, and it was in competition that the 350 best showed its high power to weight ratio. Scrambles ace Jeff Smith won 500cc World championships in 1965 and 1966 on special competition versions.

Not only were B40 based machines competition winners, they were also popular — and some of these are still in service with the British army.

The B40's competition peak was probably in 1968 when three of these machines, entered by the army, were in the only British team to survive the International Six Days Trial at San Pellegrino, Italy, finishing well up in the Silver Vase contest. The army B40s rest on their laurels today, awaiting replacement by the Can-Am two strokes.

A weakness of these machines was their energy transfer ignition system, which could be the source of some problems.

The SS90 model differed from the standard machine in that it had chromed mudguards, a seven inch front drum brake, and firmer shock absorbers.

Engine tuning was limited to an 8.75 to one compression ratio, a one and one eighth choke Amal carb and a larger inlet valve — yet this was enough to give it the edge over the standard 80mph Star.

The SS90 is very similar in appearance to the sister machine, the SS80 250cc model — just as the two standard machines were similar. Experts could see that the standard machines differed only in that the 350 had bigger wheels and brakes, heavy duty front forks, larger petrol tank and cylinder fins that cover the pushrod tube.

These famous BSA singles soldiered on until 1966 when the 250cc Starfire appeared along with the 441cc Shooting Star.

OWNER'S STORY

Robust and easily maintained

Owen Wright's B40 SS90 has the distinction of having been rebuilt in his bedroom — but he had to take off the handlebars and engage the help of his sister to get it down the stairs.

Just as the BSA single represents many aspects of the traditional British motor cycle, Owen is representative of the hard core of enthusiasts who will undertake any work on a machine anywhere to keep it on the road.

The bedroom rebuild was limited to new gaskets, new paint on the frame and general tidying up. It was promised an engine overhaul after covering an estimated 90,000 miles. The long term aim is to get the machine in as-new condition.

Owen, from Countesthorpe, Leicester, is East Midlands Branch Secretary of the BSA Owners Club. "I regard club life and rallies to be the backbone of motor cycling. I am not interested in polished concours machines so much as practical, standard bikes used every day," he says.

My bike is used daily and averages about 130 miles every week — including attending various club events. It will cruise two-up, with camping gear, at a steady 65mph, and return a fuel consumption of about 70mpg.

"Vibration has loosened the oil pump before, but this is easily fixed, and my tax disc and accessories tend to disappear — usually on motorways. Its good points are that it is robust, easily maintained, with performance and economy."

Spares for the bike are obtainable — thanks to a BSA owners' club scheme operated by Malcolm Hawkins, of Cricklade, near Swindon. The £1 per year club fee gives members the opportunity to buy from a large stock of spares.

The club is now moving towards manufacturing their own spares — with the aim of keeping all BSAs on the road.

BSA Bantam D1

Once Britain's best-selling motor cycle, with around a million made between 1948 and 1972, the ubiquitious BSA Bantam was really one of the spoils of war.

When the shooting stopped and BSA's armament contracts dried up, the factory's top brass saw a big future for a utility light-weight based on a successful German two stroke.

The basic 123cc engine-gearbox (52mm x 59mm bore and stroke) of the D1 Bantam was in fact a dead ringer of a DKW power egg with clutch and flywheel magneto juxtaposed. With little experience of the two stroke market, BSA started with a batch of export engines in March, 1948. A complete bike was announced three months later.

A WSK of the same origin gave Poland a share of post-war reparations. And while the Bantam became synonymous with Britain's domination of motor cycle markets, only a privileged few set eyes upon the DKWs in the cellars of the now flattened BSA factory at Small Heath, Birmingham.

The irony that the original DKW factory, at Zschopau, East Germany, is now the home of MZ, one of the lowest priced two strokes available in the UK, will not escape students of the rise and fall of the British bike industry.

Although the Bantam underwent many changes, with 123cc, 148cc and 174cc versions, the engines were always built at BSA's satellite factory, in Redditch, Worcestershire, where early editions acquired the pale green paintwork they shared with 500cc Sunbeam in-line twins.

Launched with a rigid back end, at a basic price of £60, the Bantam soon acquired plunger rear suspension as an extra. Standard and de luxe versions with battery lighting and electric horn instead of a pipsqueak hooter, catered for most tastes.

Customers had the choice of green, chrome or aluminium painted wheels. Accessories included a rear carrier, which had a tendency to crack mudguards if overloaded, and extremely effective legshields.

Low running costs and remarkable reliability made the Bantam a winner with organisations running messenger fleets. And red-painted Bantams on which GPO telegram boys made their deliveries became almost as familiar as pillar boxes and London buses.

A competition version with raised fish-tail silencer and a decompressor in the alloy cylinder head

One of a million Bantams made between 1948 and 1972, this D1 is an ex-GPO marathon machine and still in the restoration process.

Over 24 years the Bantam power output rose from 4 to 14bhp.

maintained BSA's sporting reputation. And engine tuners all over the world were not slow to discover that the comparatively gutless D1 (it produced a mere 4bhp at 5,000 rpm) had a lot of potential.

In 24 years, the output of production Bantams went up to 14bhp but tuners like George Todd got a lot more from them. Special flywheels and heads were fitted to innumerable racing versions. This humble but versatile machine was responsible for the formation of the Bantam Racing Club and subsequent Formula Bantam event.

Brian Stonebridge was perhaps the most successful of the pioneer Bantam scramblers, but John Draper and Dave Rowland both came close to winning the Scottish Six Days Trial on rock-bashing specials.

While technically minded enthusiasts will always associate the baby BSA with Wico-Pacy electrics and troublesome splines for concentric gearshift and kick-starter levers, others will recall that British moto cross ace Graham Noyce is just one of the many former schoolboy scramblers who cut their teeth on Bantams!

Specification — BSA Bantam D1

ENGINE: Air cooled, single cylinder, two stroke. Bore and stroke 52mm x 58mm. Capacity 123cc. Compression ratio 6.5 to 1. Iron barrel. Alloy head. Amal carburettor.

TRANSMISSION: Geared primary drive. Single roller rear chain. Multi-plate clutch. Three-speed footchange gearbox. Overall ratios 22.0, 11.7 and 7.0 to 1.

ELECTRICS: 6 volt Wico Pacy or Lucas generator. Direct lighting (rectified battery lighting extra). 6in headlamp.

CAPACITIES: 1¾ gallon petrol (16 to 1 mixture).

EQUIPMENT: Kickstarter, centre stand, spring saddle (dualseat extra), bulb horn and toolbox.

WHEELS: Steel rims with fabricated hubs. Tyres 2.75 x 19in front, 3.00 x 19in rear.

BRAKES: 5in. drums front and rear.

SUSPENSION: BSA spring telescopic front fork. Plunger rear springing.

DIMENSIONS: Seat height 27in, ground clearance 4¾in, wheelbase 50in, overall length 77in, weight 155lbs.

MANUFACTURERS: BSA Motor Cycles Ltd, Armoury Road, Small Heath, Birmingham 11.

OWNER'S STORY

Paddled off in second gear to start

A local historian who splits his spare time between digging for antique bottles and fettling a growing collection of Bantams, young Kevin Steel was little more than a twinkle in his father's eye when BSA's most famous tiddler first saw the light of day.

From Braybrooke, Northamptonshire, Kevin is a production planner in the packaging trade. He paid £35 for what is now the best of his four Bantams but says: "I've still got a lot of work to do on my D1 so there is not much point in taxing it. My ambition is to restore it to concours condition.

"It was always lying in the road and had no oil in the gearbox but it took a year to persuade the owner to part with it. The bike was actually an ex-GPO Bantam. It took over a year to find a pair of second-hand springs for the plunger rear suspension. The old springs had rotted completely. I spent a small fortune on penetrating oil to get them out.

"The D1 was released from GPO duty in 1962. It had literally been all over the country and was in a sorry state. It has cost me £220 to put right so it is no surprise to see that some Bantams are now fetching as much as £300.

"It is so easy to start that you can literally paddle it off in second gear. The centre stand is a bit weak, the gear pedal has miles of movement, and the brakes are not really adequate for modern traffic.

"My silencer is not correct for the year. It has the right outlet but the body should be shorter. I am also looking for period pannier frames and a windscreen. Then I'll get cracking on my other Bantams."

BSA A10 Golden Flash

A solid and speedy six-fifty twin, the A10 Golden Flash introduced by BSA in 1949 was a very nice touring machine which became a firm favourite with the sidecar fraternity.

Originally available with a rigid frame, it was offered with plunger rear springing a year later and with a swinging arm back end in 1959.

Unlike the 500 Model A7 BSA twin, which followed the Triumph idea of separate rocker boxes bolted to the cylinder head, the 646cc A10 (70mm x 84mm bore and stroke) engine had an integral box.

The one-piece rocker box was tidier, more oil tight and much stronger. It formed part of the heavy cast iron cylinder head and the result was very robust.

The strength of the top half was offset by the weakness of the original cylinder block flange. Adequate enough for low compression pistons (6.5 to 1) on early models, cracking of the thin flange was responsible for a number of disasters when compression was stepped up.

A spate of sports versions led to the adoption of a thicker base flange for the cast iron cylinder barrel in 1958 — the last year the A10 was available with plunger back end.

More cosmetic than anything else, BSA's plunger springing was supposed to give two inches of up and down movement at the rear wheel. In practice, the undamped plunger springs gave about one inch of movement.

This was undoubtedly better than a solid back end and because the layout provided ample anchorage for sidecar connections, the advent of the swinging arm did not send the charioteers into ecstasies.

They need not have worried. Once the geometry was sorted out, the A10 continued to pull chairs as well as ever. The faith of BSA employees in their products was reflected in the vast number of A10 outfits parked outside the Small Heath factory. In a way, the A10 became a sort of status symbol for family men who still enjoyed a turn of speed.

On solo gearing, the Flash was good for about 90mph. It started to go quicker after Gene Thiessen broke world records at Bonneville Salt flats with a souped up A10 and BSA development department stepped up compression.

An increase in cylinder fin area helped cooling but the change to swinging arm suspension was accompanied by the loss of the duplex primary chain, with tensioner under the bottom run, which was an attractive feature of the early models.

Lead-copper big-end shells and a plain phosphor

Restored A10 of 1950 vintage.

bronze main bearing on the timing side, remained unchanged throughout the 13 years the A10 remained in production but, along with other models, it acquired an Amal Monobloc carburettor in 1955.

Although the gearbox had a tendency to whine in third, cog-shifting was nice and sweet.

The front brake of the early Flashes was the envy of lesser mortals. It was an eight-inch drum, with removable core plugs, presumably to let air in to keep the linings cool in dry countries. A polished alloy backplate completed the distinguished appearance of the brake.

Capable of cruising at just over 70mph with a chair, the A10 was not a thirsty beast. A careful driver could get 50mpg at 50mph.

One of the popular combos hit by the advent of the more sociable, less tiring, more economical, and better handling Mini, the A10 cost £223 12s 3d in 1950, when new chair prices were under £100.

A dualseat put £3 on the price. Beige paintwork instead of black cost another £3 while the refinement of a propstand, quite a handy accessory for parking 425lb of top quality metal, added 15 shillings to the price!

Specification — BSA A10 Golden Flash

ENGINE: Air cooled, twin cylinder, pushrod, overhead valve four stroke. Bore and stroke 70mm x 84mm. Capacity 646cc. Compression ratio 6.5 to 1. Cast iron cylinder and head. Plain big end bearings. Amal carburettor.

TRANSMISSION: Duplex primary and single roller rear chain. Multi-plate clutch in oil. Four-speed footchange gearbox. Overall ratios (solo) 11.41, 7.77, 5.36 and 4.42 to 1.

ELECTRICAL: Lucas gear driven magneto with auto advance and retard. Lucas chain driven 45 watt dynamo with 6 volt 13 amp hour battery. 7in. headlamp.

CAPACITIES: 4 gallons petrol, 5½ pints oil.

EQUIPMENT: Kickstarter, spring saddle (dualseat extra), centre stand, sidecar lugs, toolbox.

WHEELS: Steel rims with butted spokes and fabricated hubs. Tyres 3.25 x 19in. front, 3.50 x 19in. rear.

BRAKES: 8in. front and 7in. rear drums. Alloy backplate in front.

SUSPENSION: BSA front forks with springs and hydraulic damping. Plunger rear springing.

DIMENSIONS: Seat height 29in, ground clearance 4½in, wheelbase 54¾in, overall length 85in, weight 425lbs.

MANUFACTURERS: BSA Motor Cycles Ltd, Armoury Road, Small Heath, Birmingham 11.

OWNER'S STORY

Collector and renovator side-by-side

The carefully restored 1950 A10 Golden Flash owned by BSA devotee Richard Berry is an outstanding example of how British machines were evaluated during the economic inflation of the seventies.

"I paid £500 for it," said Mr Berry, director of a family do-it-yourself and building supplies business at Sudbury, Suffolk, "and I think this was a very reasonable price in 1978."

John Lee, a neighbouring toolmaker who was restoring bikes long before it became a fashionable pastime, did not even dream of such a figure when he rebuilt the same A10 he originally bought in Billericay, Essex.

"I paid £10 for it in 1973. It was in a very poor state and I expected to spend a few bob doing it up but I never dreamed of selling it for £500. It's just crazy the way prices have soared. Now that the clowns have muscled in, you can pay £150 for a wreck."

Although Mr Lee originally bought the A10 for his own use, he has a collection of a dozen different British machines and when Mr Berry made a bid for the machine, he let it go.

"I'm more of a collector than a renovator," explained Mr Berry. "Because my father got into mischief with a number of bikes, I didn't actually own one until I was 27. My first love was a C15 BSA Starfire and my mother almost disowned me.

"When I bought the Flash, I was like a kid with a new toy. It ran beautifully and I did 500 miles in two weeks. It is still on sidecar gearing. If I found a suitable chair I might be tempted to use it as a combo."

While the engine was completely rebuilt, the frame stove-enamelled and many damaged parts replaced, an interesting restoration note is that most of the black paintwork was sprayed with aerosols.

The A10's weak cylinder block flange was strengthened in 1958.

BSA Gold Star

Immortalised by a fantastic string of sporting successes, the post-war BSA Gold Star was undoubtedly the greatest and most versatile pushrod single the British industry ever produced.

The last 'Goldie' was built in 1962. But the legendary Beezas which once dominated the Clubmans TT races were descendants of a breed designed in the mid-thirties.

The first modern Goldies were the ZBs and BBs, with rigid frames or plunger rear springing. The first clubman racers were the CBs, followed by the DBs and DBD series. But the story began before the war.

After burning their fingers at the 1921 TT, with six blow-ups from six starts, BSA kept out of racing until 1937 when Wal Handley was persuaded out of retirement to blast a prototype round the Brooklands track, near Weybridge, Surrey.

Those were the days when the British Motor Cycle Racing Club awarded a gold star lapel badge to anyone who lapped the concrete oval at over 100mph in a race. The new 500 BSA went round at 107.57mph. And a great dynasty was born.

Although the Brooklands winner was powered by an iron engine running on dope, it was the forerunner of the alloy-engined beauties which, from 1938 onwards, sported the Gold Star emblem.

Available in road or competition trim, the original M24 Goldie had a 496cc (82 x 94 mm bore and stroke) engine. It was a slow revver easily identified by a split pushrod tunnel integral with the alloy head and cylinder, and a frame similar to the side-valve M20s which became the only BSAs produced during World War Two.

After the war, the B32 Goldie was a modified B31 350 for trials and scrambles. It was followed by a B34 with the same stroke as the B32, the new 499cc engine (85 x 88 mm) forming the basis of a model destined to stun the racing scene and reap handsome profits for the factory at Small Heath, Birmingham.

An outstanding example of a sports bike developed from a humble roadster, the Goldie gave the ride-to-work clubman a golden opportunity to race on a shoestring budget. It was comparatively inexpensive and combined the best of pre-war and post-war thinking. The powerful bangers created by Roland Pike retained the bottom half of the Empire Star designed by Val Page in 1935.

With high compression piston, reversed gear pedal, and close ratio gearbox, the Goldie was perfectly adapted to regulations for the ACU's first venture into production racing — the Clubman's TT intro-

BSA Gold Star — Britain's greatest and most versatile push-rod single.

duced in 1947. Ironically, the bike proved so successful that it finally killed the golden goose.

After winning the 1949 350 Clubman's, BSA bosses got the taste so strongly that ZB Goldies soon monopolised the 350 class. And while a 500 version announced in 1950 took a little longer to worry the Norton Inters and Triumph GPs, the breakthrough came in 1953.

Eddie Dow, a newcomer to racing after long experience with army ISDT teams, daringly demonstrated the improved handling of a new duplex frame with swinging arm suspension. Fastest in practice, he shattered Geoff Duke's four-year-old lap record as he forced his BSA into second place. Then he fell off at Laurel Bank.

Roland Pike, a former Rudge racing wizard, was responsible for the massive finning of the new CB engine. He fitted an Amal GP carburettor for the first time, introduced eccentric rocker spindles to reduce the weight of the valve gear, and shortened the stroke so much that the flywheels had to be turned oval to clear the piston skirt.

The Goldies became virtually unbeatable. In 1955, Eddie Dow was back on the TT rostrum, winning the 500 Clubman's. To cap it all, he won the Thruxton nine-hour race on the same bike, a DB series model with circular fly wheels and a shorter piston which proved less expensive to manufacture.

Pioneers of clip-on handlebars, and of a combined megaphone and silencer famed for its twittering sound on the over-run, BSA pushed the power of their 500 Goldies to 42 bhp at 7000 rpm.

Not content with domination, BSA wanted to paralise their rivals. The Clubmans became a BSA benefit and the top brass of Associated Motor Cycles and Triumph resented the way their own products were being blown off.

Bernard Codd, who chalked up a 350-500 double in 1956, gave the Goldie its final fling over the TT course. The ACU's excuse for stopping the Clubman's was that 1957 was the Golden Jubilee TT for pukka works bikes, but the real reason was the takeover of the races by BSA.

The 350 Goldie was dropped in 1957. And while the 500 continued to do well in moto cross, the demand for Goldies as coffee bar racers continued to justify the production of around 2,000 a year, until the fashion changed and most touring sportsmen switched to twins.

While the Goldie continued to make its mark in moto cross, the days of the big banger were numbered by the advent of lighter machines with a better power to weight ratio. Sadly, the Goldie had to go.

Specification — BSA Gold Star

ENGINE: Air cooled, single cylinder, overhead valve, four-stroke. Bore and stroke 85mm x 84mm. Capacity 499cc. Compression ratio 8.8 to 1. Light alloy sleeved barrel. Amal TT10 carburettor.

TRANSMISSION: Single row primary and secondary chains. Multi-plate wet clutch. BSA four-speed gearbox with needle bearings. Close overall ratios: 7.92, 5.99, 4.96 and 4.52 to 1.

ELECTRICAL: Lucas racing magneto with manual control and integral waterproofing.

EQUIPMENT: Folding kickstarter, straight through exhaust system, dualseat and centre stand.

CAPACITIES: Two gallon petrol tank. 5½ pint oil tank.

WHEELS: Steel rims WM1 front, WM3 rear. Dunlop tyres 3.00 x 19 in. front, 3.50 x 19in. rear. Alloy rims extra.

BRAKES: Single sided drums, 8in. front, 7in. rear. Special 190mm front brake extra.

SUSPENSION: Telescopic front fork, swinging arm rear. Shockers with enclosed springs.

DIMENSIONS: Seat height 31in, ground clearance 5in, wheelbase 56in, weight 356lbs.

MANUFACTURERS: BSA Motor Cycles Ltd, Armoury Road, Small Heath, Birmingham 11.

BSA pushed the power of their 500 Goldies to 42bhp at 7,000rpm.

OWNER'S STORY

Change the carb and see a transformation

One of a handful of enthusiasts who specialise in Gold Star spares, George Prew bought his 1962 DBD 34GS (all engine numbers have the suffix GS) in touring trim two years ago and promptly rebuilt it to Clubman's specifications.

A perfectionist whose hobby has helped fellow owners all over the world, he spends most of his working time as a heavy goods tester for the Ministry of Transport.

"I've been a motor cyclist since I was 15," said Mr Prew at his home at Barkway, near Royston, Herts, "and I've owned a variety of BSAs, from a C11G to a B40 and a Starfire.

"My first bike was a 350 Matchless. My present ride-to-work bike is a 1976 Triumph Bonneville, with the gear pedal on the right. It was one of the 1,500 models locked in the factory during the Meriden dispute.

"I gave £600 for the Goldie. It was advertised in Motor Cycle News by Mike and Dave Hoskinson, of Bee-Bee Bros., Birmingham, but was originally registered by Eleanor Motors, in London. I am the sixth owner.

"I don't like the GP carburettor. The only reason I have it on the bike is to keep its originality. An Amal Concentric transforms the bike completely, making it easier to start and sacrificing only a few mph at the top end.

"If I ride the Goldie, I fit a Concentric. One good reason is that GP parts are getting scarce. I have a 23 tooth engine sprocket. It gives me a speed of 60 to 70mph in first and about 115mph in top.

"This means I have to slip the clutch, but a Goldie does not have to be high geared. You can get engine sprockets down to 17 teeth and make them quite docile and tractable.

"I personally prefer the 650 Rocket Gold Star twin. I have two of them. One was raced in Ireland. The other is in original condition with steel tank and Amal Monobloc carburettor."

BSA Rocket Gold Star

Last of the pre-unit construction BSA twins, the 650 Rocket Gold Star is a rare animal which, surprisingly, has yet to gain the charisma or collector's value of the more common but highly sought-after Goldie singles.

One explanation is that the sports twin never achieved any startling competition results. Another is that too many bitzas, often built after 1963, are advertised as the real thing. Buyers have been warned!

Introduced in February 1962, and dropped some 18 months later under the pretext that supplies of magnetos had dried up, the Rocket Gold Star was actually the last survivor of the famous A10 range. It was a high performance hybrid, with a Super Rocket engine in a frame similar to that of the race-bred Gold Star but without the kink on the right hand side to miss the oil pump.

As Super Rocket engines were individually bench tested, the best were earmarked for Rocket Gold Stars. The first batch was built in September 1962, starting with engine number DA10R 5958 and frame GA10 101.

Developed from the 646cc (70mm x 84mm bore and stroke) Golden Flash, introduced in 1949, the 46bhp pushrod twin featured a cast iron cylinder block and alloy head. It was fitted with Spitfire cams, Monobloc carburettor (some conversions sported

Above: Alloy head with horizontal side fins was a distinctive feature of the engine. Left: An Eddie Dow converted specimen.

an Amal GP), 9 to 1 compression ratio pistons, and siamesed exhaust pipes. An accessory manufacturer later marketed a twin-carburettor conversion.

Other components included a close ratio RRT2 four-speed gearbox and a Gold Star front fork. Touring and clubman versions were listed by BSA, with flat bars for the former and clip-ons for the latter. And both were supplied with Goldie steel tanks which nowadays fetch at least £100!

Eddie Dow, the Gold Star specialist who persuaded the factory to produce the machine, converted a number of touring models to sports trim with Lyta five-gallon alloy tanks and cast-alloy fork yokes.

No more than 1500 examples were built before they were superseded by the A65 range. No official parts list was ever printed. The only list was a typewritten sheet for the BSA with a specification like a bitza!

Specification —
BSA Rocket Gold Star

ENGINE: Air cooled, twin cylinder, pushrod overhead valve four stroke. Bore and stroke 70mm x 84mm. Capacity 646cc. Compression ratio 9 to 1. Aluminium alloy cylinder head. Light alloy connecting rods. Dry sump lubrication and double gear type oil pump. Amal Monobloc carburettor.

TRANSMISSION: Multi-plate clutch. Four speed footchange gearbox on needle rollers. Reversible pedal. Extra-close ratios (internal) 1.0, 1.10, 1.32 and 1.75 to 1.

ELECTRICAL: Lucas magneto with manual auto-advance and retard. Separate chain driven 6 volt dynamo. 7in headlamp.

CAPACITIES: 4 gallons petrol. 5½ pints oil.

EQUIPMENT: Folding kickstarter, dualseat, clip-on bars, rev counter, centre stand, steering damper, siamesed exhaust.

WHEELS: Steel rims (alloy extra) with Dunlop tyres 3.25 x 19in front and 3.50 x 19in rear.

BRAKES: 8in drum front (light-alloy 190mm version extra), 7in drum rear. Finger adjustment.

SUSPENSION: BSA hydraulically damped telescopic fork. Swinging arm rear with hydraulically damped spring units adjustable for load.

FRAME: Cradle type of all-welded construction.

MANUFACTURERS: BSA Motor Cycles Ltd, Armoury Road, Small Heath, Birmingham 11.

OWNER'S STORY

Classic thunderbike that tingles the fingers and motors to 117mph

Roger Grundy, from Market Harborough, Leics, has been hooked on BSAs for over ten years. And the 650 Rocket Gold Star he bought in 1976 is a real goer.

A founder member of the East Midlands branch of the BSA Owners Club, he also owns a 250 Starfire and a 175 Bantam to which he plans to hitch a Watsonian Bambi sidecar to take his dog to rallies!

His wife, Bobbie, is also a BSA fan and a leading light in the social activities of one of the most lively branches of the club. Originally listed at £370, the Rocket Goldie had five previous owners before Mr Grundy bought it for £450.

According to Mr Grundy, a good genuine example can fetch between £1,000 and £1,500. But although he swears by BSA, which he claims are cheaper to run than any modern bikes, he is refreshingly honest about the snags of a thunderbike which was among the best of British.

"It was pretty tatty when I got it, with oil and insulating tape everywhere, and I went to a lot of trouble to strip it and build it up again," says the present owner, whose BSA has a non-original alloy rear wheel and open spring shockers.

"I'm not anti-Japanese but I'm not really interested in modern multis. I've tried a few and I prefer the simplicity of post-war British machinery."

Keen on camping, Mr Grundy and his wife have ridden as far as Scotland and Holland without a hitch. "In ten years, we've never broken down further than pushing distance from home.

"The Rocket Gold Star was not really built for modern traffic. The brakes were probably OK in 1963 but are inadequate today.

"It weighs about 420lbs and it took me 1½ years to discover the knack of raising it on the centre stand by heaving on the kickstarter pedal. Steering lock is very limited and clip-ons are a problem with a vertical twin renowned for vibration. It takes only a few miles to make my fingers tingle.

"Magneto ignition is a mixed blessing. It makes the bike easier to start. But as no ignition key is fitted, anybody can start it. Tickover is not exactly in the gas engine class. And as you can't get out of first gear until you reach about 30mph, the clutch has to take a lot of slipping.

"My bike has odd rear suspension struts so the handling leaves a little to be desired. The top speed is in the region of 117mph but I seldom take it over 80."

BSA Fury

The story of the BSA Fury is the story of the "classic" bike that never was.

The double overhead camshaft 350cc twin was announced in October 1970 when the BSA-Triumph Group took the covers off their 1971 22-strong model range.

Shown to dealers and Press at a lavish London launch, the Fury was partnered in Triumph form by the Bandit which was identical apart from the design of the petrol tank and dual seat. Both bikes also appeared dressed with high rise "moto cross" type exhaust systems to appeal to the American market in SS — Street Scrambler — guise.

As the first all-new British middleweight bike since the 1958 Ariel Leader, the 350 twin was hailed as a major step forward for the BSA-Triumph Group which was being criticised for not being adventurous enough. The orders flooded in but the

Left: the 350 Fury, a revolutionary roadster that never made full production. Above: route of the chain that drove double overhead camshafts is clearly seen in this engine side view.

company was not ready to meet them. If they had, perhaps the BSA-Triumph name would still be alive today.

As it is the Fury and Bandit faded away into history without every going into production. Only a handful of the original test and show machines still survive to tease the enthusiast with thoughts of what might have been.

A power output of 34bhp at 9,000rpm was claimed for the 350 which was earmarked to sell at £380. An extra £21 would buy an electric starter which was mounted behind the forward inclined cylinder barrel.

Twin 26mm Amal Concentric carburettors fed the engine which had a bore and stroke of 63 x 56mm and a compression ratio of 9.5:1. The one-piece steel crankshaft was supported by one ball and one roller bearing and had the crankpins set at 180 degrees to each other to overcome the problem of vibration.

A chain from the left hand side of the crankshaft drove the overhead cams and a 0.375in duplex chain transferred the power from the engine to the multi-plate clutch. Both the five-speed gearbox and kick starter were mounted in "Japanese" fashion on the left hand side of the motor.

A dry weight of 345lbs was claimed for the bike which employed a lightweight duplex cradle frame of similar design to those used on the Daytona, Trident and Rocket Three race machines. Wheelbase was 58.5in and the seat height was set at 30.2in.

Specification — BSA Fury

ENGINE: Air cooled, twin cylinder, double overhead camshaft four stroke. Bore and stroke 63mm x 56mm. Capacity 349cc. Compression ratio 9.5 to 1. Aluminium barrels and head. One-piece 180 degree steel crankshaft. Twin Amal 26mm concentric carburettors.

TRANSMISSION: Multi-plate clutch in oil. Duplex primary and final chain. Five-speed gearbox with overall ratios 17.1, 11.84, 9.03, 7.37 and 6.39 to 1.

ELECTRICS: 12 volt battery, and twin coils with crankshaft mounted Lucas alternator.

CAPACITIES: 2½ gallons petrol, 6½ pints oil in frame tube.

EQUIPMENT: Kickstarter, dualseat, direction indicators, rev counter. Electric starter available as an extra.

WHEELS: Steel rims with conical alloy hubs. Tyres 3.25 x 18in front, 3.50 x 18in rear. QD sprocket.

BRAKES: 8in twin leading shoe front, 7in single shoe rear. Snail cam adjusters.

SUSPENSION: Telescopic fork with two-way damping and internal springs, swinging arm with hydraulic shock absorbers and exposed springs.

DIMENSIONS: Seat height 30.25in, ground clearance 6.9in, wheelbase 58.5in, overall length 79.5in, weight 345lbs.

MANUFACTURERS: BSA-Triumph Group.

OWNER'S STORY

Quick but with a lot of mechanical noise

One of the few surviving examples of the BSA Fury was displayed in the Birmingham showrooms of L H Vale Onslow. The machine was rescued from the factory on the eve of its closure together with a Triumph Bandit stablemate.

The Bandit — which was registered in 1969 and used as one of the original road test machines — has been sold but offers of £2,000 plus were needed before the famous Birmingham motor cycle dealers would consider parting with the Fury.

Although the Fury had no engine internals a complete spare engine sat in the workshop.

Mr Peter Vale Onslow, a director of the business and son of the founder Len, believed the machine was the actual show model displayed at the original dealer and press launch in October 1970.

A cloud was already hanging over the future of the BSA Triumph Group when the factory launched its 1971 model range with pomp and lavish ceremony. The press and dealer launches were held on consecutive days kicking off at the London Hilton Hotel and transferring the following night to the Royal Lancaster.

"It was impossible to believe that the factory was having any financial trouble. I have never seen anything like it before or since," said Peter.

Pride of the new range was the 350 dohc twin and orders flooded in from the dealers. Peter placed

The new 8-inch twin leading shoe front brake and 7-inch single leading shoe rear drum were common to the majority of machines in the 1971 range.

The new front forks were also fitted to every other bike in the range apart from the Bantam and Daytona 500. Over 6½ inches of travel was claimed for telescopic forks which featured two way damping.

Indicators were fitted as standard to the 350 twin which was as stylish as anything being produced by the Japanese factories.

When one of the rare examples of the bike came into Motor Cycle News' hands in 1973 it was suggested the high revving engine used fifth gear as an overdrive.

An extract from the road test reads: "Handling was impressively taut as befits a sporting 350 but for my liking the handlebars could have been shorter and straighter.

"The engine was smooth but some vibration could be felt through the footrests. Frankly, the ride was a disappointment. My expectations had been higher but is it fair to criticise after a ride on a neglected four-year-old bike? Obviously not and in the back of my mind I felt the unit had tremendous potential. . ."

So would the Fury and Bandit have been successful if they had gone into production? Unfortunately the answer has to be one of pure conjecture.

orders for 120 BSA-Triumph machines and 40 of them were for the new 350 although he admits he did have his doubts about it.

"The learner could not buy it because of the capacity. And for the same sort of money you could buy a Bonnie for although they announced a massive price increase for the new 650 the old 650s we still had in our showrooms were selling at £395," he said.

"The rolling chassis itself was superb but I feel they should have used it to house 250, 350 and 500 engine units of the Tiger 100 type. The factory did not have the up to date equipment to compete with the Japanese in producing a dohc machine."

Although not officially unveiled until late 1970 Peter caught several previews as the early prototypes were put through their paces. "I had seen them running about Birmingham about six months before the London show launch," he said.

Recalling his own experiences of riding the Bandit, he remembers that it was quick but mechanically very noisy.

350 Douglas Mark V

Too often overshadowed by the presence of the Official Receiver at the Bristol factory, the 350 Douglas Mark V was a classic example of a good bike which failed to make a fortune for its makers.

It was nevertheless the most popular of the post-war production Duggies, all of which were powered by a 348cc (60.8mm x 60mm bore and stroke) transverse flat twin originally designed as a wartime portable generator motor.

Of the 11,576 reputedly produced between 1946 and 1957, when Douglas (Kingswood) Ltd., stopped making bikes, 3,113 Duggies were Mark V versions with torsion bar rear suspension and leading link front forks.

Introduced immediately after the war as an alternative to a rigid frame, the Douglas spring frame was devoid of damping but the swinging arm pivot was so close to the gearbox sprocket centre that rear chain tension was virtually constant.

Technically ahead of its time, the torsion bar frame first appeared on early T35s, or Mark 1 models, distinguished by the word Douglas on the ohv rocker box covers. Only a few of these models survive.

How did it work? Spring steel torsion bars were inside the bottom frame tubes. At the front, the bars were spined into special lugs. At the back, forged links on plain bearings joined the bars to the swinging arm. The twisting action limited movement in the same way as normal coil springs.

Torsion bars were also envisaged for the front fork but discarded in favour of square section multi-rate springs with two-way oil damping. With parallel links to isolate brake torque, the forks remained popular with sidecar grass track racers long after production ceased.

Shaft drive, a feature of the Endeavour transverse twin unsuccessfully launched by Douglas in 1934, was dropped in favour of bevel gears to transfer the drive from the gearbox mainshaft to the chain sprocket via a transmission shock absorber. Unlike a BMW, the kickstarter was normally situated on the right of the machine and could be operated when straddling the bike.

While the Mark III retained a toolbox under the saddle and the Mark IV a cast aluminium waffle box silencer under the gearbox, both the Mark IV and the Mark V sported twin cast aluminium pear-shaped tool boxes with extensions to carry pillion footrests hitherto mounted on the swinging arm.

The adoption of longer exhaust pipes, with Burgess silencers as standard equipment on Mark IV Sports

Every inch a concours winner, this restored Douglas Mark V shines right down to the engine castings.

69

and Mark V, made it necessary to redesign the previously excellent cast aluminium centre stand. Narrower than before, the new stand was notoriously unstable. Ironically, the famous waffle box was offered as an optional extra.

The basic model cost £235 in 1951 with a saddle, but the last models, built in 1954, were fitted with a dual seat, oil filter, and air filters for the carbs.

Into big time trials like the Scottish Six Days with David Tye and Ted Breffitt, and encouraged by the excellent steering and suspension of their roadsters, Douglas had a crack at the Clubmans TT.

This led to the celebrated 90 Plus, a racing version good for 10,000 to 11,000rpm with special cams, racing magneto, Amal TT carburettors, close ratio box, and a magnificent nine inch diameter front brake.

Engines which failed to produce 25bhp at 6500 rpm on the test bench were set aside for the 80 Plus, a similar machine in touring trim. But the Douglas racing venture was eclipsed by the all-conquering BSA Gold Stars.

Although Dave Chapman won a clubmans race at Silverstone, the highest placing in the Island was fourth in 1950. The racing Duggies, tuned by Eddie Withers and pre-war star Freddie Dixon, were pushed to 31bhp, giving them a top speed of nearly 110 mph, but they were never fast enough to beat the Goldies.

These torsion bar Duggies should not be confused with the Douglas Dragonfly, a single carburettor job which came out in 1955 with Reynolds-Earles forks, conventional rear suspension and fixed headlamp nacelles.

OWNER'S STORY

I once made the mistake of changing one

A building worker on the vast new town complex of Milton Keynes, Charlie Summers paid only £35 for the 1951 Douglas Mark V with which he has twice won concours d'elegance first prizes.

"That was in 1969" recalls Mr Summers, a former electrician from Wolverton, Bucks, whose excuse for buying the machine is that he once made the mistake of parting with a similar model.

"I owned a Mark IV Douglas in 1958. I exchanged it for a 197cc DMW my father rode to work while I did my national service in the Army. It was the worst thing I ever did. When I saw this advertised I jumped at it.

"It was in restorable condition so I rebuilt the engine and treated the cycle parts to a complete polychromatic blue paint job. I fitted new wheels, repaired the back mudguard, and eventually replaced the Burgess silencers. You can't buy them anymore."

"A box of spares was part of the deal, including a 90 Plus gearbox which I exchanged for a replacement Lucas magdyno so the bike doesn't owe me anything."

Among the bike's accessories are a luggage carrier and chromed crashbars which, like the silver and plated tank panels, were originally optional extras.

Although Mr Summers won concours prizes in 1970 and 1977 at London Douglas rallies, he has had less success with a Mark III model for which he paid £200. Both bikes are kept under dust sheets.

"I don't ride them very often, and don't go fast. I get about 60mpg at 50 to 55mph but my old Duggie was good for about 78mph.

"I bought it in Northampton for £45 in 1958 after the gearbox of my pre-war BSA Empire Star disintegrated. Although some of my pals tried to put me off the Douglas, my only problem in two years was a spot of clutch slip."

Standard equipment included the pillion pad, crude but a nice gesture.

Specification — 350 Douglas Mark V

ENGINE: Air cooled, horizontally opposed, overhead valve, twin cylinder four-stroke. Bore and stroke 60.8mm x 60m. Capacity 348cc. Compression ratio 7.25 to 1. Cast iron cylinders and heads. Alloy rocker boxes. Amal carburettors.

TRANSMISSION: Car-type clutch to four-speed footchange gearbox with bevel gears from mainshaft to single row secondary chain. Overall ratios: 15.54, 9.6, 7.05 and 5.57 to 1.

ELECTRICAL: Lucas magdyno with manual advance and retard. 6 volt, 9 amp hour battery. 7in headlamp.

EQUIPMENT: Kickstart, spring saddle, pillion pad, cast alloy centre stand, cast alloy tool boxes.

CAPACITIES: 2 gallon petrol tank, 5 pints oil in sump tank.

WHEELS: Steel rims with fabricated steel hubs, 3.25 x 19in tyres front and rear.

BRAKES: 7in. diameter drums front and rear.

SUSPENSION: Leading link front forks with springs and hydraulic damping. Torsion bar rear springing with box section swinging arm and links to rods housed in bottom frame tubes.

DIMENSIONS: Seat height 29in, ground clearance 6½in, wheelbase 56½in, overall length 86in, weight 382lbs.

MANUFACTURERS: Douglas (Sales and Service) Ltd, Kingswood, Bristol.

Francis Barnett Cruiser

Cruiser, as a name for Francis Barnett's top of the range model in the early 1960s could not have been more apt — the Cruiser 89 twin was one of the last of the solid style British two strokes.

Heralded as a luxury lightweight in 1961, the 250cc machine was a cruiser indeed by modern standards. A top speed of about 70mph certainly did not qualify this bike as a sportster, but it did have cheapness, simplicity and that thoroughly British style to recommend it.

Francis and Barnett Ltd had used Villiers engines from an early date, and the Cruiser 89 employed the Villiers 2T engine at first, but later the more powerful 4T model.

The smooth twin was added to the range of two stroke singles which once consisted of five other

Left: Finished in green and white with a gold lined tank, the Francis Barnett Cruiser 89 was one of the last solid style British two-strokes.
Above: Villiers 4T engine that replaced the old 2T.

machines — ranging from the unorthodox 150cc Fulmar (similar in appearance to the Ariel Arrow), the 150cc Plover, 200cc Falcon and Cruisers 80 and 84 which used 250cc single cylinder engines.

Before the demise of Francis Barnett, their Cruiser 89 offered practical motor cycling for only £183 18s 4d and a road test of the time showed that no less than 102mpg was possible at 30mph.

The twin did not offer a big improvement in performance compared with its 250cc stablemates, but the engine was quite a buzz-box for its day and gave good acceleration at the expense of top speed.

That engine could certainly take some revving — the first Press road test of the 89 showed it would do about 23mph in first gear, nearly 40mph in second, about 52 in third and pull a maximum of nearly 72mph.

An oval front down tube was a feature of the frame, the rest of which was built up with looped tubes attached to a pressed steel centre section. There was a front stand to aid removal of the wheel, while the number plate had to be removed before the back wheel could be taken out. A chromium plated tank and white wall tyres were once listed as extras.

The Cruiser was produced at the Birmingham base of James motor cycles, where Francis Barnett had been installed by the parent company, Associated Motor Cycles. Both Francis Barnett and James ceased to exist in the mid-1960s.

Greeves Sports Twin

During its seven-year career from 1959 to 1966, the 250cc Sports Twin became the most popular single model ever produced by Greeves, including their more famous moto cross and trials bikes.

Equipped with the ubiquitous Villiers 2T two-stroke engine, with its well undersquare dimensions of 50 x 63.5mm bore and stroke, the Sports Twin borrowed the distinctive die-cast aluminium beam frame from its competition stablemates. This, together with the leading link front fork which featured rubber-in-torsion springing and damping by Girling hydraulics, gave the model a distinctively spartan appearance.

It was no bad thing, in an era when many manufacturers using Villiers power-plants for their lightweights were experimenting with ponderous and

Left: Functional lines in an era when cumbersome enclosures were popular was a hallmark of the Sports Twin. Above: The alloy beam downtube was claimed to be stronger than a tubular structure.

often ugly enclosures to distinguish their bikes. Greeves claimed that the die-cast I-beam downtube was stronger and more resilient than a conventional tubed assembly — although the Sports Twin's rear subframe relied on tubular construction.

The 2T's peak output, running on a compression ratio of 8.2:1, was 15.5bhp at 5,500rpm, and this was sufficient to give the four-speed bike a cruising speed of around 60mph. Performance may not have been sensational, but the Villiers engine was noted for its mellow, vibration-free running and the familiar yowl from its exhaust system. An advantage of the leading link forks was that they declined to dive under braking, which was provided for by six-inch units front and rear. The bike weighed about 270lbs, and carried a three-gallon fuel tank.

Code named the 25DB, the first Sports Twin ran from 1959 to December 1960, after which it was retitled the 25DC. Both bikes offered the unusual radially finned hubs, as used on the competition machines, as an alternative to the standard unfinned hubs. But full width hubs were fitted to all 25DC Mk IIs, which began life in late 1964 and continued through to the model's end in the summer of 1966. This variation was equipped with the 4T Villiers engine, which gained an unfortunate reputation for seizures.

By the time increased Japanese competition led Greeves to abandon production of road bikes in 1966, more than 1,700 of the unassuming but popular Sports Twins had been made.

James Captain

For what in retrospect seems a singularly unexciting design, the James Captain enjoyed a career that was long-lived by the standards of many of the mundane two-strokes that thrived briefly in the forties, fifties and sixties.

Launched in 1949 as a three-speed, rigid-framed economy model by the Greet factory, it passed through plunger and swinging arm variations, gained an additional ratio in the gearbox, was powered at different times by Villiers and AMC units, and blossomed towards the close of its life into a sports option complete with flyscreen, dropped bars, rear-sets and a reversed gear pedal!

Unsophisticated though it may have been, the Captain obviously had the ability to captivate buyers by doing most things reasonably well, if achieving

Left: This 1957 version of the Captain has well-valanced mudguards and Villiers power unit. Above: A sculpted tank and rearswept exhaust pipe were among racy features of the Sports Captain.

nothing very dramatically, before its demise was spelt out by the great AMC crash of the early sixties.

The 197cc single-cylinder Villiers unit powered the first models. A plunger rear end was adopted soon afterwards, while the swinging arm design arrived in 1953. By 1958 an improved version of the Villiers 9E unit was employed, although the long-stroke 59 x 72mm bore and stroke dimensions remained the same. Hydraulically damped Girling rear units replaced the previous undamped James legs, while detail modifications included a change from rather primitive V-grooved steering head races to spherical ball seatings for greater contact area. The top speed of these models was about 60mph, with cruising speeds in the 45 to 55mph bracket. Yet fuel consumption could reach 100mpg.

Writing in 1959, one road tester fulsomely praised the Captain's performance, handling, steering, braking, sweet clutch, comfort, and easy starting — yet the frequent use of maximum acceleration in second gear resulted in chain stretch and the need for constant adjustment!

The Sports Captain weighed some 260lbs, and indicated speeds in its four ratios were in the order of 30, 45, 55 and 65mph. Seventy mpg was available at a steady 60mph, while the bike accelerated to 50mph in 12.3 seconds.

There was nothing revolutionary in the AMC engine that was fitted to the Captain for some model years. This 199cc unit even had a similar long-stroke configuration to the Villiers unit, actual bore and stroke measurements being 59 x 73mm. Its slotted transfer ports had the endearing habit of trapping the piston rings, and really it was not enough to save the Captain from an inglorious end.

350 Matchless G3LS

Direct descendant of the military 350 Matchless coveted by the privileged Don R's of Dad's Army, the G3LS was one of the most gentlemanly singles the British industry ever produced.

Don R's were the soldiers for whom the tedium of square bashing, Naafi queuing and other service routine was relieved by biking duties. And those lucky enough to get a Matchbox pioneered the Teledraulic fork.

Although BMW had telescopic forks before the war, London's Associated Motor Cycles factory was the first in the British industry to adopt this now universal design for post-war Matchless and AJS models.

Like many demobbed riders, the civilian version put on weight at such an alarming rate that its performance eventually suffered, but the G3 remained a popular slogger until it went out of production in the mid-1960s.

The G3 was the basic WD Matchless, with girder forks, developed from a pre-war machine with cast-iron cylinder head and coil valve springs.

The G3L was introduced halfway through the war. It sported the famous teles and was appreciably lighter — hence the suffix L for Lightweight.

The G3LS was the spring frame version, announced in 1949 with swinging arm back end and slim shockers. Early AMC shockers were replaced by the more sophisticated jampots in 1951.

Too good to be produced economically, the imposing jampots were eventually dropped in favour of proprietary units which did the job almost as well and kept the AMC shareholders happy.

Pioneers of a policy of integration unkindly dubbed badge engineering, AMC streamlined production so much that differences between Matchless and AJS singles from the same plant were finally reduced to the name on the tank.

The two makes could originally be distinguished by the position of the magneto — in front of the cylinder on AJS and behind on Matchless versions — but adoption of the same crankcase castings with the mag in front on both makes even put paid to that.

The dynamo was always inaccessibly sandwiched between the engine plates. And when separate magnetos and dynamos went out in favour of alternators on the end of the crankshaft, only the badges differed.

Similarly the essential difference between the 347 cc G3LS Matchless and 16MS AJS (69mm x 93mm

Highly sought after by renovators, bikes like the 350cc Matchless G3LS were the cream of Britain's ohv touring singles.

79

'Gentlemanly' describes the G3LS, a direct descendant of military G3s.

bore and stroke) and the beefier 498cc G80LS and Model 18S (82.5mm x 93mm) was the bore size.

Crankcase castings were the same and the 350s were even fitted with 500 flywheels in which only the balancing differed. And the incredible inertia of those heavy flywheels was part of the charm of the Plumstead singles.

Almost invariably a first prod starter, the long stroke 350 was a plodder which would almost literally climb the side of a house in bottom cog. It was not fast, but it was nearly impossible to stall it.

Always renowned for mechanical quietness, the AMC singles acquired unique wire-wound pistons which permitted closer clearances and reduced piston slap when cold.

The method unfortunately proved useless when hot. It did not allow sufficient space for expansion and most owners invested in a new piston with conventional rings.

Hairpin valve springs were employed from 1949 onwards and an alloy cylinder head was adopted for both touring and competition versions in 1951. On 350s, the inlet valve was bigger than the exhaust.

Until 1954, the crankshaft was supported by main bearings of the same size. In 1955, the diameter of the drive side bearing was increased and the front forks were also stiffened.

Inevitably, with the same frame for 350s and 500s, the touring bikes became too sluggish. Designers tried to tweak them, with high lift cams, better valve gear and improved lubrication, but they fought a losing battle.

Trials and moto cross versions outlived the cooking models. While an alloy primary case replaced, the notoriously leaky early tin case, and an AMC gearbox superseded the Burman box in 1957, the willing 350 was doomed and made way for a unit-construction bored-out 250.

Specification — 350 Matchless G3LS

ENGINE: Air cooled, single cylinder, pushrod, overhead valve four stroke. Bore and stroke 69mm x 93mm. Capacity 347cc. Compression ratio 6.5 or 7.5 to 1. Cast iron cylinder. Alloy head. Hairpin valve springs. Amal carburettor.

TRANSMISSION: Multi-plate clutch. Single roller primary and rear chains. Four-speed foot-change gearbox. Overall ratios 15.4, 9.9, 7.6 and 5.8 to 1.

ELECTRICAL: Chain driven magneto ignition with manual advance/retard. Separate 32 watt dynamo charging 6 volt battery for lights. 7in. headlamp with twin parking and pilot lights.

CAPACITIES: 3 gallons petrol, 4 pints oil.

EQUIPMENT: Kickstarter, prop and centre stands, dualseat.

WHEELS: Steel rims with full width hubs, straight pull spokes, adjustable taper bearings and full width hubs. Quickly detachable rear wheel with pull-out spindle. 3.25 x 19in. tyres front and rear.

BRAKES: 7in. drums front and rear with shim adjusters.

SUSPENSION: AMC Teledraulic front fork and swinging arm rear with AMC shockers.

DIMENSIONS: Seat height 31½in., ground clearance 5½in., wheelbase 55¼in., overall length 86¼in., weight 376lbs.

MANUFACTURERS: Associated Motor Cycles, Plumstead Road, Woolwich, London SE18.

OWNER'S STORY

Weight is the handicap

A trials enthusiast and former RAF fitter who serviced aircraft for the H-bomb nuclear tests on Christmas Island in the Pacific more than 20 years ago, Maurice "Mo" Bird regards his 1955 G3LS Matchless as an investment.

"I gave £70 for it in 1975. It had 45,600 miles on the clock and was a bit tatty but completely original. Although I've not completed the restoration, I've already been offered close to £1,000 for the machine."

A self-employed hydrovane compressor specialist from Isham, near Kettering, Northants, Mr Bird has owned a wide variety of trials and touring bikes, including four Matchlesses. "My first was an ex-WD 350 rigid G3, registered in 1948, on which the saddle springs were the only hint of suspension.

"I also owned a couple of 500s, including one with a sidecar. I've never been able to explain the reason, but I've always liked the name Matchless better than AJS.

"I like the slow thumping noise of a British banger. They give the impression they will never wear out and run so slowly that you wonder why they didn't stop ten minutes ago.

"Handling is better with the spring frame but weight was always a handicap. Acceleration was poor and top speed was nothing to shout about. But once you get the 350 wound up to 50 or 65mph it will go for evermore.

"The chaincase is a bit primitive, with only one screw to hold the oil, but the filler acts as a level hole so that you can't overfill the case.

"Quickly detachable wheels, low petrol consumption, and superb comfort for rider and pillion passenger offset the snags," added Mr Bird, a former solo and sidecar trials rider on Greeves and Bultacos, who still competes in pre-1965 four stroke trials with a 1958 500 BSA Gold Star.

Norton ES2

It is a back-handed tribute to pioneers of the most respected name in British motor cycling that the basic engine layout of the Norton ES2 pushrod single remained in production for no less than 40 years.

Although more sophisticated than the prototype overhead valve Norton of 1922, the last of the line in 1962 retained the 490cc dimensions of the original long stroke (79mm x 100mm) Model 18 engine.

An economical and slow revving slogger, the ES2 was something of a shirehorse for solo or sidecar work. It wasn't fast but, in its traditional black and silver, it symbolised the dignity of a marque which really was the best of British.

Introduced in 1928, five years after the Model 18, the ES2 is believed to have started as an export special, with a better frame similar to CSI overhead

Above: The engine of the ES2 is so tall that rocker boxes are almost hidden in a recess under the tank. Left: This ex-RAC slogger was built in 1955 but looks fresh from the showroom and is still in regular service.

camshaft models to cope with more power than standard.

Conceived at a time when Norton were as keen on proving their products between Lands End and John O'Groats as they were on TT racing, the ES2 achieved an enviable reputation for low petrol consumption.

The long stroke engine inhaled and burned petrol in a miserly manner. And although the claimed power output was never more than 22bhp at 4200rpm, it was quite common for owners to get 90 miles to the gallon.

Never good for much more than 75mph, the ES2 was probably at its best doing 60mph at 3500rpm in top. Heavy flywheels gave the engine tremendous torque.

Plunger rear springing, available before the 1939-45 war, was retained until 1954 when a decline in sales prompted the Bracebridge Street, Birmingham, factory to convert the cradle frame of ES2 to swinging arm suspension.

The factory's annual production was never more than 6,500 bikes. But, following the adoption of the Featherbed frame for Norton twins, with frames built at the Reynolds factory, Norton sales slumped to 70 bikes a week.

The switch from plunger to swinging arm worked wonders and the ES2, with compromise front fork trail of 2¾ ins suitable for solo or sidecar work, enjoyed a new lease of life.

Specification — Norton ES2

ENGINE: Air cooled, single cylinder, pushrod, overhead valve four stroke. Bore and stroke 79mm x 100mm. Capacity 490cc. Compression ratio 6.4 to 1. Cast iron cylinder. Alloy head. Amal carburettor.

TRANSMISSION: Multi-plate clutch. Single roller primary and secondary chains. Four-speed footchange gearbox. Overall ratios 12.7, 8.41, 6.31 and 4.75 to 1.

ELECTRICAL: Lucas Magdyno with manual ignition advance/retard. Six-volt 12 amp hour battery. 7in. headlamp.

CAPACITIES: 3¼ gallons petrol, 4 pint oil.

EQUIPMENT: Kickstarter, exhaust valve lifter, dual seat, centre stand.

WHEELS: Steel rims with full width alloy hubs. Tyres 3.25 x 19in. front and rear.

SUSPENSION: Norton Roadholder telescopic front fork. Swinging arm rear springing with Girling shockers.

DIMENSIONS: Seat height 30in, ground clearance 6in, wheelbase 56in, overall length 85½in, weight 384lbs.

MANUFACTURERS: Norton Motors Ltd, Bracebridge Street, Aston, Birmingham 6.

OWNER'S STORY

Perfect running is like a bloodhound lapping milk!

Edward Lewis, a Northampton shoe manufacturer whose footwear is worn by most motor racing champions, enjoys the quiet dignity of riding to work on his 1955 ex-RAC Norton ES2.

Owner of a variety of Nortons, including Dominators and Manx racers, he is a former racing driver who rode a 1926 350 Sunbeam round Britain to raise money for cancer research.

"I am not an authority on Nortons but the age of post-war engines can be determined from prefix letters. They began with C in 1948. The letter I was skipped so J engines were made in '54.

The bike he rides most is the ES2 bought in good shape in 1975. It does not have the original engine but the replacement is of the same vintage, with the prefix letter K for the engine number.

After changing the magneto of his ES2 at his home in Blisworth, Northants, Mr Lewis admitted he was puzzled by a mysterious misfire. "I took the mag off and put it back and the engine ran perfectly — like a bloodhound lapping milk!

"They're slow. Handling is only adequate and cannot be described as good. Their real charm lies in being a relaxing and pleasurable method of getting across the countryside reliably and economically."

Although big end bearings occasionally succumbed to the thumping of the long stroke engine the ES2 was extensively used by RAC patrolmen, with and without box sidecars.

A merger with Associated Motor Cycles in 1952 led to considerable integration, including the Burman gearbox common to AJS and Matchless, but, apart from the Manx racers, Norton singles in Featherbed frames did not come out until 1959.

Just how many ES2s were built is not known. What is evident is that a plan to change the engine capacity to 496cc (82mm x 94mm) was frustrated by the Second World War but a 500T trials version of the long stroke engine achieved considerable success.

Mr Lewis has never been in the motor cycle industry. But he was once involved in a motor engineering project in which a Manx engine was used to develop inlet ports.

During his sporting career he raced Riley, Lotus and BMC cars. Now, his bikes range from a pipsqueak 1922 225cc Ivy to a ripsnorting 1974 850 Norton Commando in production racing trim.

"Starting the Commando is a real rupture job," said the greying enthusiast who bought the bike (above) one of two built for Isle of Man travelling marshals, from an NVT Wankel tester.

Norton Jubilee

The Jubilee's parallel twin engine with well over-square bore and stroke dimensions was a product of Bert Hopwood's fertile mind.

Futuristic or ponderous? The Jubilee's styling, with the deeply valanced front mudguard and comprehensive enclosure of the rear end, aroused much dispute as to its worth.

The Norton Jubilee, launched in late 1958 to mark the company's formation sixty years previously, was unusual among post-war British 250cc four-strokes in that if offered multi-cylinder motorcycling to quarter-litre enthusiasts.

Designed by Bert Hopwood, whose influence swept so resoundingly through the industry in these years, the Jubilee featured a twin-cylinder 'high camshaft' pushrod engine of 60 x 44mm bore and stroke dimensions. The engine and transmission was built in unit, and was compact and handsome, matching a deeply valanced front mudguard, a fully enclosed rear chain, and partial enclosure of the machine's rear end. For a 250 it looked sophisticated but heavy, as indeed it was at some 330lb dry.

Breathing through an Amal Monobloc carburettor, the Jubilee compressed its mixture at a ratio of 8.75:1 inside its alloy heads, resulting in a peak output of 16bhp at 7,750rpm. Primary drive was by a ⅜in, duplex chain to a four-speed gearbox.

Pressure from Associated Motor Cycles, the parent group that had merged with Norton in 1953, led to certain frame and brake parts that were not of pure Norton lineage being incorporated into the Jubilee. A pressed steel front downtube was married to twin top tubes, while the 18in. wheels carried brakes of 6in. diameter.

The Jubilee was good for a top speed in the mid-seventies, although the engine had to be generously buzzed to reach such rates. A standing quarter mile time of some 20 seconds would be regarded as laughable from a modern 250, but was by no means slow for a well-equipped 249cc model more than two decades ago. A realistic cruising speed was probably no more than 55 to 60mph, but one huge advantage the Jubilee held over contemporary 250s was its miserly rate of fuel consumption — 80mpg and more was readily obtainable.

But despite its potential appeal, the Jubilee suffered the same fate as many British 250s. Its production span lasted less than ten years, in an era when many British bikes enjoyed careers of two or three decades. One of the victims of the final collapse of AMC, and that company's takeover by Manganese Bronze Holdings, the Jubilee had just too little character to survive. The British will always be remembered for their big bikes, not their lightweights.

Norton International

A faint blue haze from the exhaust of a Norton International was the hallmark of a healthy example of the last of Britain's single overhead camshaft touring "bangers."

Notorious for the hyper-sensitive oiling system of its vintage valve gear, it was an enthusiast's machine with all the character of a hand-built thoroughbred.

Survivor of a breed going back to the 'twenties and 'thirties, the Inter was a built-to-order model which, in its final Featherbed form, was virtually a single ohc Manx Norton. The big difference was the long stroke engine the Inter retained until a shortage of special big-end bearings swayed the management of the Bracebridge Street, Birmingham, factory, to drop it from the range.

So few were built that the manufacturers did not include it in the catalogues of the mid-'fifties and there were many disappointed customers when it was announced that the 1957 models were the last of the line.

Old-fashioned but solid, with steel flywheels instead of cast iron, the engine of the post-war Inters were basically the same as the updated 500 designed by Arthur Carroll in 1931.

Apart from minor improvements, most of them in the rocker lubricating and sealing department, the 490cc (79mm x 100mm bore and stroke) single cylinder motor was almost unchanged for a quarter of a century.

Offspring of the original CS1 overhead camshaft TT winner created by Walter Moore in 1927 before he joined NSU and gave the Germans a replica of his early chimney stack engine, the Inter was a racing-cum-touring job. It packed a powerful punch but, with a maximum engine speed of no more than 6,000 rpm it was no match for the high-revving BSA Gold Stars which eventually ousted it from clubmans racing.

A top speed of 98mph was reached during electronically timed tests at MIRA, near Nuneaton, Warwickshire. And while this was quick enough to satisfy pre-motorway road burners, the Norton was no longer fast enough for serious racing.

The bevel drive to the overhead camshaft was similar to that of the double ohc Manx racers and the condition of oil-sealing felt washers on the adjustable rockers was critical. Never renowned for mechanical quietness, the all-alloy motor developed a more pronounced rattle if a well regulated oil supply, denoted by the characteristic blue haze from the exhaust, was not carefully maintained.

Norton International — for the enthusiast.

Sporting exposed hairpin valve springs under the deeply recessed petrol tank, where part of the offside frame was flattened to clear the cambox, the tall engine of the Model 30 (Model 40 was the 350cc version) bristled with adjusters and breathers for the lubrication system.

Because oil was prone to drain from the tank into the crankcase, generally due to a speck of dirt on the pressure release ball valve, many owners fitted a tap on the main feed pipe. Fastidious enthusiasts kept an eye open for the slightest discoloration of their rocker pads. Overheating invariably preceded a messy appearance while tiny feeds to the valve guides, on the exhaust side in particular, had a nasty habit of getting carboned up.

With alloy engine plates, a better big-end bearing than the equivalent pushrod ES2, a 10TT Amal carburettor, butterfly filler caps for oil and petrol tanks, and a wingnut instead of the normal knob for the steering damper, the Inter retained a hint of its racing days. But there was another curious link with its competition background.

Although close ratios were standard, the gap between first and second gear was fantastic! If an owner wanted a higher bottom gear, he had to insert a Manx cog and do away with the kickstarter until a special request from Daytona, where bump-starting was not allowed, prompted production of a special gear which enabled the Americans to fire up on the pedal.

Only minor improvements made the 490cc engine virtually unchanged over 25 years

Specification — Norton International

ENGINE: Air cooled, single cylinder, overhead camshaft four stroke. Bore and stroke 79mm x 100mm. Capacity 490cc. Compression ratio 7.12 to 1. Bevel drive from crankshaft to camshaft. Hairpin valve springs. Amal carburettor.

TRANSMISSION: Five-plate clutch with rubber shock absorbers. Single roller primary and secondary chains. Four-speed footchange gearbox. Overall ratios 10.8, 6.18, 5.1 and 4.64 to 1.

ELECTRICS: Lucas Magdyno with manual advance/retard, 6 volt 12 amp hour battery and automatic voltage control. 7in. headlamp.

CAPACITIES: 3½ gallons petrol, 5½ pints oil.

EQUIPMENT: Kickstarter, dualseat, centre and prop stand, chromed mudguards, rear wheel driven speedo, pillion footrests.

WHEELS: Steel rims with alloy hubs. Tyres 3.00 x 19in. front, 3.25 x 19in. rear.

SUSPENSION: Norton Roadholder telescopic front fork. Swinging arm rear springing with Girling shock absorbers.

DIMENSIONS: Seat height 31in, ground clearance 5½in, wheelbase 56in, overall length 86in, weight 394lbs.

MANUFACTURERS: Norton Motors Ltd, Bracebridge Street, Aston, Birmingham 6.

OWNER'S STORY

Inspires confidence at any speed

A keen collector who has got into the routine of rebuilding a classic bike every winter, Jim Bussey is a farmer who reckons motor cycling is more fun than flying.

"I held a pilot's licence for five years but I got bored with it. I get more enjoyment out of bikes but look forward to the day road tax is included with the price of petrol.

"I bought the Norton and a pair of Vincents from a Scott fanatic who wanted the money to treat himself to a vintage Scott, said Mr Bussey, from Holcot, near Northampton.

In addition to the 1957 Norton International, which he obtained in bits, he has two vintage Triumph singles, two pre-war Ariel Square Fours, a Vincent Black Shadow and a Vincent Comet.

His son is a local scrambler who does occasional stunts with a CZ. And Mr Bussey, who survived a hand grenade accident during the war, has been a motor cyclist for over 40 years.

"The Norton took me a whole winter to do up. It needed new valves and guides but I like its strength and simplicity. Look at the amount of metal on the kick-starter clamp.

"I've always liked Nortons. I rode 16H side valvers before I got discharged from the Army but the Featherbed Inter handles much better. It inspires tremendous confidence at any speed. I've had 95mph out of it. I doubt if it will go any faster but it took me a long time to get the hang of the big gap between first and second gears."

Norton Dominator 650 SS

Capturing public imagination from the start, Norton's Dominator 650 SS won Motor Cycle News' Machine of the Year competition for two successive seasons and made third place in 1964. It first took the title in 1962, the year of introduction, reflecting popularity of the Norton as a fine touring bike with a distinctly sporting side to its character.

The 650 SS has its origins in the Norton model 7 of 1947, a 500cc vertical twin. Shortly after this, all Norton twins took the "Dominator" tag, and certainly lived up to this name with their roadholding once the famous "featherbed" frame was adopted. The frame went slimline in 1960.

Up until the 'sixties, buyers had the choice of either the 88 500cc machine or the 600cc 99, and then both models became available in higher compression SS forms. The 650 Sports Special was offered in addition to these machines.

But Norton were apparently unprepared for the invasion by Japanese bikes. The parent company, Associated Motor Cycles, was wound up at the end of 1966 and Villiers Engineering took over to form Norton Villiers — but this did not stop the flow of Dominators from the factory.

The 650 SS went on until 1968, when the 750cc Atlas, which had been introduced in 1963, was also dropped. The Dommie may have died, but it lived on in spirit — the 750 Commando engine was basically a tilted Dommie lump.

The success of the Commando is another story — it was MCN Machine of the Year 1968 to 1972 — but it is interesting that it needed an isolastic frame to dampen the vibration. The 650 SS was not plagued with the same vibration, but had a comparatively sweet-running engine, linked to a slick gearbox.

With 115mph as a top speed, the 650 was not out-performed by the Commando — and yet Norton stressed the 650 SS as a touring machine in their advertising.

Though the Dominator's competition history is not to be confused with a Domi-racer derivative, it was raced with some success, high point being when a Dommie won the Thruxton 500 mile event.

That the engine internals were special to the 650 and not taken from the 600cc model 99 was a point made by Charlie Rous when he road tested the 650 SS in 1962.

"If there was ever a steel fist in a velvet glove then that's the lastest M1 mile eater from

Dominator 650 SS, one of the last old-style Nortons to be made before Commando production started in 1968.

Nortons..." he began the test. He said it was the fastest bike Motor Cycle News had tested after achieving maximum revs in top gear, 6,800 rpm, and an indicated 120mph in those pre-restriction days.

The "power packed" machine was said to churn out a claimed 49bhp. The test praised the Norton's mellow exhaust note, handling, brakes and lights. Handling was said to be perfect at all speeds — helped by the use of racing style Avon tyres. The brakes anchored the 398lb bike from ton-plus speeds without fade.

This was a bike "for the rider who still likes his motor cycling in man sized proportions". All that for £322.

Specification — Norton Dominator 650 SS

ENGINE: Air cooled, overhead valve, twin cylinder four stroke. Bore and stroke 68mm x 89mm. Capacity 647cc. Compression ratio 8.9 to 1. Twin Amal monobloc carburettors.

TRANSMISSION: Rear chain ⅝in x ¼in., front chain ½in. x .305in. Gear ratios 11.6, 7.57, 5.52 and 4.53 to 1.

ELECTRICS: Lucas magneto ignition with manual advance and retard. Alternator with rectifier and 12 volt 6 amp hour battery. 7in. headlamp.

CAPACITIES: Petrol 3.6 gallons, oil 4½ pints.

EQUIPMENT: Kickstarter, dualseat, centre and prop stands, chrome mudguards, speedo and rev counter, pillion footrests.

WHEELS: Steel rims with tyres 3.00 x 19in. front and 3.50 x 19in. rear.

BRAKES: 8in. front drum, 7in. rear.

SUSPENSION: Norton Roadholder front forks, swinging arm rear with telescopic shock absorbers.

DIMENSIONS: Seat height 31in, ground clearance 6¼in, wheelbase 55½in, overall length 85in, overall width 26in, weight 398lbs.

MANUFACTURERS: Norton Motors Ltd, Bracebridge Street, Birmingham.

Showroom Dominator 650 SS of 1962, sporting siamesed exhaust and traditional tank.

OWNER'S STORY

Performs competitively with modern Japanese bikes

It took about six months of asking before the previous owner of Alan Shepherd's Dominator 650 SS agreed to sell. That was in 1974, and since then the machine has proved to be fast and reliable, and understandably now a highly-prized possession.

Alan, of Aspull Moore, Wigan, fell in love with the Dommie at first sight, and such is his keenness to preserve it, he has removed the original tank, with distinctive chrome flashes and replaced it with another Norton tank painted in traditional colours.

Reason is he does not want to take the risk of dropping the bike and spoiling an irreplaceable feature of the machine — and it could be argued that the painted tank is an improvement on the original.

Other departures from standard are the instrument bracket and headlight — but the essential character of the machine is retained. The alloy rims were optional equipment when the machine was new. A standard Dommie would have its speedometer recessed in the headlight shell and rev counter on a bracket.

Alan has had to do very little to the Norton to keep it on the road. He has simply fitted new silencers and adjusted the tappets along with routine servicing. The bike is out every weekend to rallies and meetings.

The machine features 12 volt electrics, introduced in 1963/64, and a sports magneto and alternator. Earlier models had dynamos, while later ones had alternators and coil ignition.

"It is certainly fast," said Alan. "I have had 90mph with throttle to spare, but the engine is 14 years old and must be getting tired, so I don't ride too fast. I have never even had the head off to check it, and I don't want to touch it if it is going well — and nothing has ever fallen off!

"I think the bike is still competitive in performance to modern Japanese bikes. I don't like disc brakes, and my twin leading shoe front brake does very well. It is not expensive to run, being British, but the twin concentrics give about 55 mpg. With fairly flat bars, it has a very comfortable riding position."

Among the bikes that Alan has owned in the past were a BSA A7 Star and an A10 Super Rocket, and he rates the Dommie a better bike than the Super Rocket.

He is restoring a Norton Big Four 600cc sidevalve single, and almost needless to say, is a member of the Norton Owners' Club.

Alan founded The British Motorcycle Owners Club in 1974, and the one branch now has its maximum 150 members. He hopes other branches will be started in other parts of the country.

Norton Dominator 88

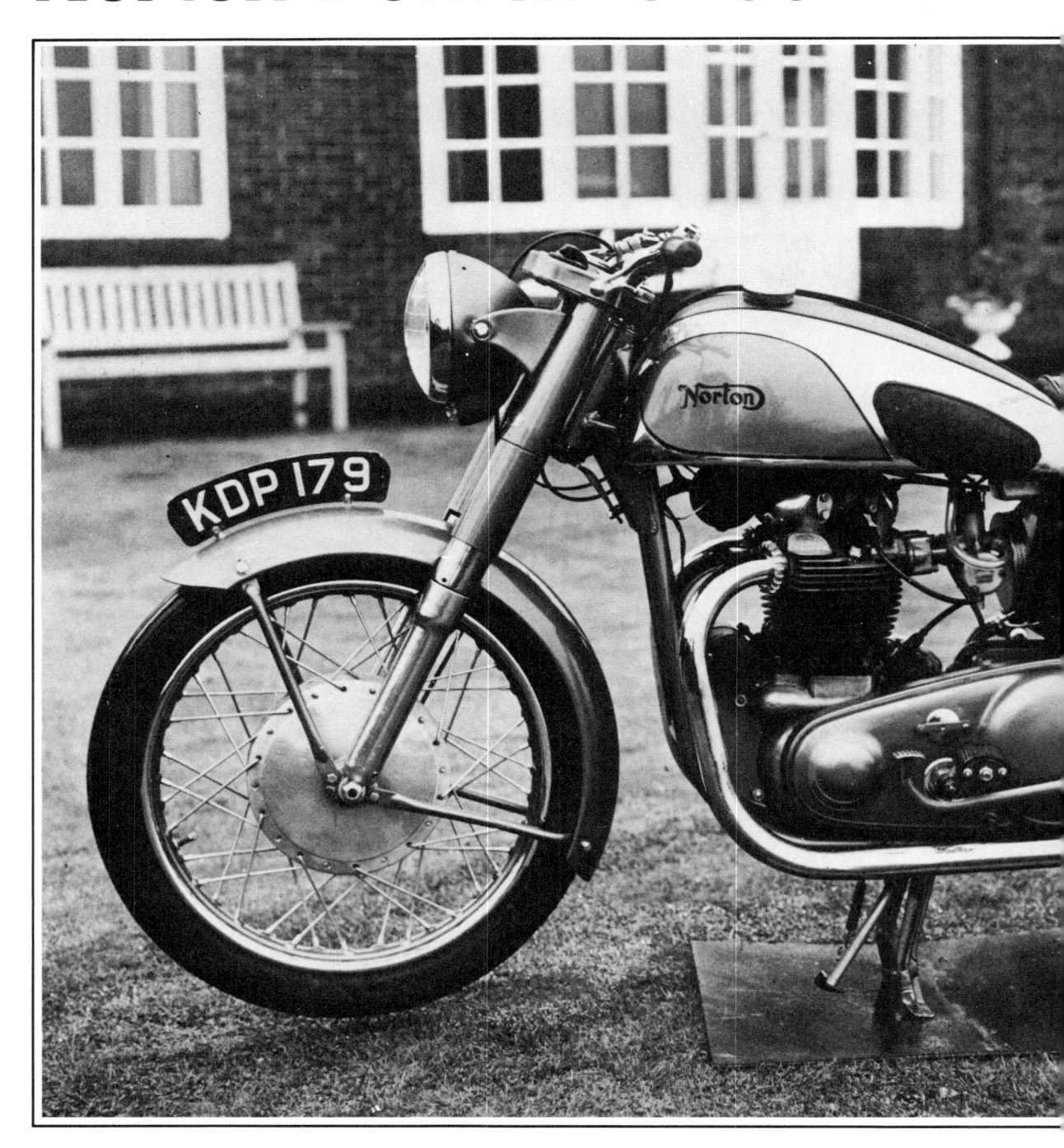

Too broad in the beam for real comfort and a bit lacking in steering lock, the Norton Dominator 88 was nevertheless a superb touring bike which revolutionised the concept of good roadholding on two wheels.

The Dommie, as it became universally known, was the first production roadster to sport the race-bred Featherbed frame. And the superlative steering of this 500 twin set the standard by which its contemporaries were judged.

Originally for export only, the Model 88 was introduced in 1952 and came on the home market a later. It was a fairly docile sports job with an alloy head on the engine Bert Hopwood designed for the Bracebridge Street, Aston, Birmingham, factory in 1949.

The frame was something else. Brainchild of Ulsterman Rex McCandless, who subsequently received royalties on his patented design, this remarkable chassis was destined to form the backbone of all sorts of specials. Sensation of 1950, when Geoff Duke chalked up his first TT win, the Featherbed gave a new lease of life to the Manx Norton racers on which the rider sat much further back.

The attractive styling of the Dommie's tank and seat could not be faulted but, because these components sat on top tubes the same width as the racer's, the riding position was too wide for all but those with really long legs. Duke once rode a modified Featherbed Dommie in a national trial where his attempts to stand on the pegs in sections nearly made him bow-legged for life!

While the spacious and wide tubular structure enabled the engine to squat well forward to help weight distribution, and gave a good wide anchorage for the swinging arm pivot, the crossing-over of the frame tubes behind the 64 degree steering head was a weak point. Northern scrambler Ted Ogden gave a memorable demo when he raced an early Featherbed. His wheelbase grew longer at every jump until the crankcase grounded and he gave up. The frame did not break, but it is significant that later Dommies sported gussets behind the steering head and the offending tubes were sleeved for strength.

Clean lines of a 1954-55 Dominator 88. Note stiffening gussets for the cross-braced steering head tubes of the Featherbed frame, peardrop silencers, dynamo in front of the engine, magneto behind the cast-iron cylinders and cut-out button under the seat. Dangling wire is for the missing rear number plate.

The Norton factory did not make the frames. They came from Reynolds, the tubing manufacturers, where the limited output of a frame building section ensured that the demand for Dommies was never satisfied.

Early 88s had a bolted rear sub-frame. A fully welded structure was adopted from 1954 onwards but the wide tank rails survived until 1960 when Norton's top brass finally recognised that not everybody has long legs and proudly announced a Slimline version with the top tubes squeezed closer together.

From the start, the handling of the Dommie was so good that, like the Mini a few years later, it was capable of much higher speeds than the delightfully sweet 497cc long-stroke engine (66mm x 72.6mm) was able to give it. Of conventional layout, with a cast iron cylinder block, low compression pistons, a single carburettor, and fairly woolly cams on a camshaft in front of the crankcase, the engine was so well engineered that it was only a matter of time before the call came to pep it up.

Tuned twins for Daytona races led to hot cams and high compression pistons on all 88s from late 1955. A really substantial bottom end, with shell big-end bearings and ball and roller mains, along with a race-bred gearbox, made the Dommie a real goer.

OWNER'S STORY

Appealing because it's so well made

Director of an engineering company who views contracts for oil rig modules and conveyor systems in the Middle East as part of the daily grind, Jim Rishworth is a perfectionist who gets his kicks from rebuilding British bikes.

"I had a Dommie in the mid-fifties. It was virtually the same as the 1954-55 model I have rebuilt. My wife and I did a lot of continental touring in those days. Our longest trip was about 2,000 miles.

"The bike always handled well, either solo or two-up, but it was Norton engineering that appealed to me. It was always an easy bike to work on because it was so well made.

"I got this bike in 1976. It cost me £240, which is about £24 cheaper than when it was new. The machine came from Leeds, and had 44,000 miles on the clock, which could be genuine. I did nothing to the bottom-end but treated the engine to a top-end rebuild.

"Although the bike was complete, it had to be stripped and repainted. The rear mudguard was not original so I obtained a replacement from the London firm of Hamrax. It was all fairly plain sailing. The worst part was painting the silver grey strip with red-lining down the centre of the rims. This had to be done before respoking the wheels which are fitted with the correct Avon tyres catalogued at the time.

"The only part I need to complete the machine is the rear number plate and its mounting," added Darlington-based Mr Rishworth whose next rebuild was to be a 1956 Dominator 99, the 600cc version which led to the 650 SS and the 750 Atlas before Norton, along with other members of the AMC group, slipped into the history of British biking.

Weighing 390lbs, with a wheelbase of 55½ inches, a seat height of 31 inches, and a ground clearance of 6¾ inches, the 88 enjoyed an attractive steel grey paint job and distinctive peardrop silencers.

Along with the dualseat, the three-and-a-half gallon tank was specially contoured to allow a rider to grip the knee pads but, at a time when most touring types wore long footing coats, the width between the knees made it difficult to stop coat tails from flapping in the wind.

The Dommie was the sort of bike you could thrash all day but a vibration period at around 90mph prompted the makers to use rubber mountings for handlebar clips on early 88s. Short flat bars rested on a neat speedo, ammeter, and light switch panel above the Roadholder forks.

Brakes were a match for the bike's admirable appetite for continental touring in the days when a pound sterling was still worth a quid and a rider could get a good kip in a German gasthof for ten bob but the Dommie had another endearing virtue. It was a petrol miser. Unlike twin-carb versions with bigger engines, a 500 Dommie could cruise at 60mph on the pilot jet of its Amal Monobloc and do up to 90 miles per gallon. Thinking about it puts progress into perspective.

A pristine SS version of the 1962 Norton Dominator 88 range. Models from 1960 were slimmer.

Specification — Norton Dominator 88

ENGINE: Air cooled, twin cylinder, pushrod, overhead valve four stroke. Bore and stroke 66mm x 72.6mm. Capacity 497cc. Compression ratio 7.8 to 1. Cast iron cylinders. Alloy head. Alloy con rods. Plain big-end bearings. Amal Monobloc carburettor.

TRANSMISSION: Multi-plate clutch in oil bath. Single roller primary and rear chains. Four-speed footchange gearbox. Overall ratios: 12.7, 8.41, 6.31 and 4.75 to 1.

ELECTRICAL: Lucas magneto ignition with auto advance/retard. Separate 60 watt dynamo and 6 volt 12 amp hour battery for lights. 7in headlamp.

CAPACITIES: 3½ gallons petrol, 4½ pints oil.

EQUIPMENT: Kickstarter, tool and battery cases, dualseat, prop and centre stands.

WHEELS: Steel rims with full width alloy hubs. Tyres 3.25 x 19in front, 3.50 x 19in rear.

BRAKES: 8in front and 7in diameter rear drums. Finger adjusters.

SUSPENSION: Norton Roadholder telescopic forks with hydraulic damping. Swinging arm rear suspension with two-way shockers.

DIMENSIONS: Seat height 31in, seat width 12in, ground clearance 5½ in, wheelbase 56in, overall length 86in, weight 406lbs.

MANUFACTURERS: Norton Motors Ltd, Bracebridge Street, Birmingham 6.

Panther 100

The Panther 100 is in a class of its own. For while most 'collectable' machines are built to pristine condition and rarely venture onto the highway. Panthers are seldom showpieces and most of them are in everyday use.

There's another difference too — more than half of all Panther 100s are attached to sidecars.

The Panther 100 was never a glamour bike like many of its rivals — it sold mostly as an inexpensive big bike that was ideal for pulling a chair.

The machine had its origins in the 500cc ohv

Specification — Panther 100

ENGINE: Air cooled, single cylinder, overhead valve, pushrod four stroke. Bore and stroke 87mm x 100mm. Capacity 598cc. Compression ratio 6.1 to 1. Cast iron barrel and head. Amal carburettor.

TRANSMISSION: Multi-plate clutch in oil. Single roller primary and secondary chains. Burman four-speed footchange gearbox. Overall ratios (solo) 11.98, 7.04, 5.65 and 4.49 to 1; (sidecar) 13.61, 8.00, 6.42 and 5.1 to 1.

ELECTRICS: Lucas Magdyno ignition with manual advance and retard. 6 volt 13 amp hour battery. 7in headlamp.

CAPACITIES: 3 gallons petrol, 4 pints oil (tank under crankcase).

EQUIPMENT: Kickstarter, exhaust valve lifters in head and timing case, spring saddle, front and rear stands.

WHEELS: Steel rims with butted spokes and fabricated hubs. Tyres 3.25 x 19in front, 3.50 x 19in rear.

BRAKES: 8in front drum and 7in rear.

SUSPENSION: Dowty air forks, rigid rear end.

DIMENSIONS: Seat height 28in, ground clearance 6in, wheelbase 54in, overall length 83in, weight 385lbs.

MANUFACTURERS: Phelon and Moore Ltd, Cleckheaton, Yorkshire.

Great combination — handsome 600cc Panther 100 complete with 1928 home-built sidecar.

An example of one of the later Panther 100s, brand new and posing for publicity photographs. Wonder where it is now......

single intoduced by the Phelon and Moore parent company in 1924 and which grew to 600cc three years later. This was to remain its size for 32 years when the capacity was upped to 650.

P and M had established a style in 1901 when their designers were the first to come up with the concept of making use of the power unit to replace the frame downtube. They saw that the layout saved weight and provided a very rigid structure. The system was preserved right until the firm folded in 1966.

It was the fantastic power produced in the low and middle ranges that made the Model 100 such a popular choice with sidecar enthusiasts.

Peak power from the 598cc engine is developed at between 5,500 and 5,600 rpm and peak torque is at just 3,500rpm.

The smoothness of the low down pulling power which was so ideal for the chairmen was helped by the use of a massive cast iron flywheel which weighed in at an incredible 14lbs.

Kicking over a 600cc single bore and stroke of 87mm x 100mm can be very hard work indeed, even though the compression ratio is a relatively modest 6.5 to 1, so Panther incorporated a half compression device which lifted the exhaust valve slightly half way up the compression stroke.

This is operated by lifting a lever on the right hand side timing cover which worked an auxilliary cam next to the exhaust cam. With the lever in operation the engine will continue to run at reduced power until the lever is returned.

A remarkable feature of the engine was the twin port exhaust system, adopted mainly because of the difficulties of silencing a big single of the type adequately. A single port option was however available for those who wanted to fit a left hand chair with the exhaust and silencer on the right.

OWNER'S STORY

Quarter of a million miles machine

An investment of £10 secured Fred Baggs his pride and joy — a 1952 600cc Panther 100 and double adult sidecar.

Fred, who lives in Farnborough, Hants, had owned a succession of British singles when he started courting and decided he needed a combination.

He discovered that an uncle of his girlfriend, Mary who he later married, had a Panther combo in his shed. The outfit had been standing for six years when Fred first saw it in 1971 and the speedo showed it had covered more than 190,000 miles.

He borrowed a lorry to take the outfit home, cleaned the points, filled the tank with fresh petrol and it fired first time!

Scientific civil servant Fred drove the bike for another 2,000 miles before he decided it needed a rebuild and since then has covered more than 52,000 miles using the outfit as a primary method of transport.

The engine has undergone its second rebuild and is now running as well as ever.

The chair the bike is attached to has an unusual history. It was home made around 1928 by Fred's wife's uncle who fashioned it out of ash and teak sheathed in aluminium. It's a genuine two door 'saloon' type and features a roomy boot.

"That must be the best £10 worth I've ever had," said Fred. "For that tenner I also got another bike thrown in for spares."

Fred, who is spares secretary of the Panther Owners Club, likes to look after his machine in the same way as someone buying it from new in 1952 would have done.

To him and most other Panther owners the make is very much a live one and the aim is to keep all the remaining Panthers on the road and used as everyday transport.

Royal Enfield Crusader

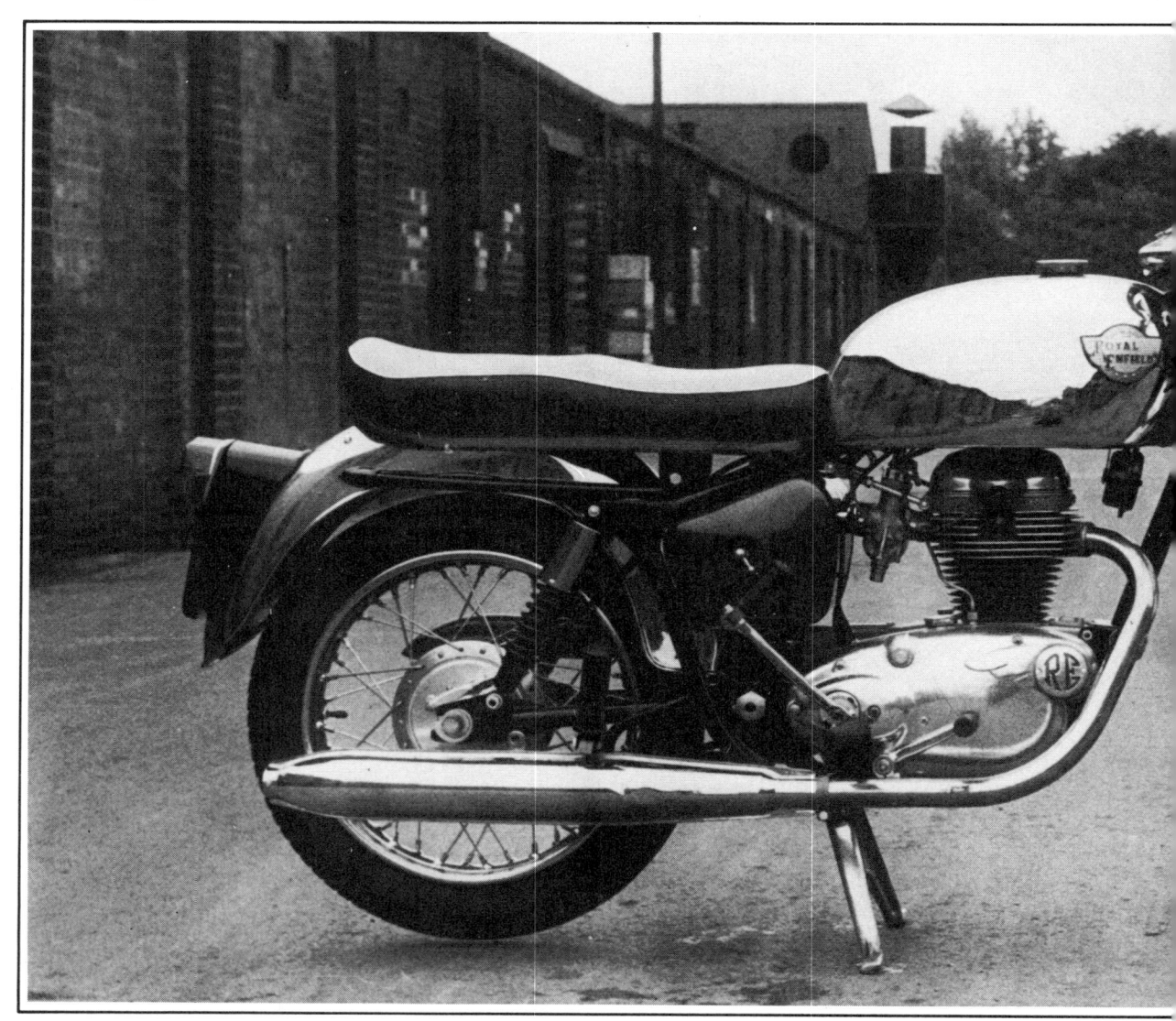

When Royal Enfield launched their 250cc Crusader at the London show of 1956 it was said to epitomise modern motor cycling. Potential buyers were lured by Enfield's statement that "all modern trends and advances have been incorporated to produce a machine which will give the rider tremendous satisfaction and pride in the knowledge that he possesses one of the most up-to-date motor cycles available".

It certainly attracted attention and set the Redditch factory off on a long line of successful quarter litre machines for the next eleven years. Ironically, it was their fascination for the class that contributed to collapse in 1967. A reputed £150,000 was spent developing a two-stroke twin world beater in road racing, masterminded by Herman Meier. The project was halted in 1965, reason being given as lack of success but the implications went much deeper.

Historians reflect on what might have happened

Above: The Crusader engine as it first appeared in 1957 with split shell, white metal big-end bearing working direct on a massive Meehanite iron crankshaft. Left: A Crusader of 1964, showing signs of influence from the Continental.

if the over-square, Crusader instigated four-stroke had been developed instead, albeit with less ambition. A four-valve version had been pencilled in for 1968.

The story of the Crusader is really the story of the engine which began life as a low performance mill of 70mm bore x 64.5mm stroke, low compression and a two-plate clutch. Approximate velocity was 70 mph.

By 1960 things were looking better with a major rehash providing a Sports model featuring high-lift camshaft, bigger inlet valve, revised rocker gear and one more plate in the clutch. And star of the 1962 range was Enfield's Crusader Super Five, which broke new ground with a five-speed gearbox and leading link forks. Claimed power output was 20bhp and speed 80 — 85mph.

A trials version was also made available, using a Sports power unit, and went on to achieve competition success in the hands of Peter Fletcher. One year later, Enfield announced their return to racing with a works scrambler. Again it was the Crusader engine that took on the role.

Though Crusaders continued in one form or another up to 1965, it was the Continental, launched at the show of 1962, which finally took over this popular little 248cc motor. It's final form was in the Continental GT, heralded as Britain's fastest 250. Chas Mortimer had one of his first professional rides on a Gander and Gray entered GT in the 1967 Thruxton 500-miler, finishing fifth in the class with his partner having averaged over 70mph for six hours.

Last of the Crusaders proper appeared piece-meal in the Enfield Olympic of 1966. The Olympic was really a means of using up as many Crusader parts as possible!

Royal Enfield 350 Bullet

Sporty enough to have been chosen by the last British team to win the World Trophy in the International Six Days Trial, the Royal Enfield 350 Bullet was the most popular machine produced by the Enfield Cycle Co Ltd, of Redditch, Worcestershire.

With a pedigree going back to the early 1930s, when the factory launched a range of ohv sports singles, the 350 Bullet in competition or touring trim continued to reign supreme until the Midlands firm folded in the mid-60s.

The early overhead valve engines were long strokes with 70mm bore and 90mm stroke, giving an actual capacity of 346cc — the same as the last of a famous line from a company whose trademark was a field gun and whose slogan was "Made like a Gun".

Still made in India, by a former subsidiary in Madras, with slightly different engine castings and carburettor, the 350 Bullet developed a modest 19bhp at 6000rpm. Top speed was between 75 and 80mph, but it would crack along all day at a steady 65mph.

Charlie Rogers, long associated with the sporting activities of a factory with a distinguished record in trials, put the seal on the reputation of the 350 Bullet when he won the 1937 British Experts trial with a rigid frame model.

In 1949, the Bullet returned with swinging arm rear suspension. It was later joined by a 500 version, with the same long stroke but a 84mm bore and heavier flywheels. And it was a combination of these engines which helped Johnny Brittain to stardom as an Enfield works rider.

Hitherto considered unsuitable for trials, the spring frame gained universal acceptance after Johnny scooped virtually every major trials award, from the 1952 British Experts before his 21st birthday to the British trials championship in 1956.

In 1953, when he was picked for the British ISDT Trophy team for the first time, Brittain and a 350 Bullet formed a vital partnership in our last success in the six-day marathon.

Along with most contemporary British bangers, the Bullet was very economical. The 350 easily gave 80mpg overall, while the 500 was good for up to 72mpg, a top speed of 90mph and the ability to chuff along in top gear down to 1000rpm.

Works 350 trials bikes were often fitted with flywheels from the 500. All-alloy engines saved weight on works machines but the position of the oil tank as an integral part of the crankcase came with unit construction.

Still active, a 1955 350cc Bullet.

Drive side of the 1955 350. Later frames were appreciably higher.

Specification — Royal Enfield Bullet

ENGINE: Air cooled, single cylinder, pushrod, overhead valve four stroke. Bore and stroke 70mm x 90mm. Capacity 346cc. Compression ratio 7.25 to 1. Cast iron cylinder and alloy head. Light alloy con rod. Amal Monobloc carburettor.

TRANSMISSION: Duplex primary chain in oil. Single roller rear chain. Multi-plate clutch. Four-speed footchange gearbox. Overall ratios 15.9, 10.35, 7.45 and 5.72 to 1.

ELECTRICAL: Lucas magneto ignition with auto advance and retard. Lighting by 70 watt AC generator and 6 volt battery. 7in. headlamp.

CAPACITIES: 3¾ gallon petrol tank, 4 pint oil tank integral with engine for dry sump lubrication.

EQUIPMENT: Kickstart, neutral selector, dual seat, centre and prop stands.

WHEELS: Steel rims with 3.25 x 19in. tyres front and rear.

BRAKES: Twin 6in. front drums, single 6in. rear drum.

SUSPENSION: Telescopic front fork and swinging arm back end.

DIMENSIONS: Seat height 31in, ground clearance 5½in, wheelbase 54in, overall length 86in, weight 370lbs.

MANUFACTURERS: The Enfield Cycle Co Ltd, Redditch, Worcs.

Originally in front of the engine, the oil tank for the dry-sump lubrication was sandwiched between the crankcase and the gearbox on post-war models. Another Enfield feature was a vulnerable-looking but highly practical oil filter housing at the bottom of the timing case.

An improved oil pump, along with an extra main bearing and extensive frame alterations, were among the changes for 1956 but the Albion four-speed gearbox with the neutral selector fitted to the gear indicator and the long gearshift pedal was fitted until the factory closed.

An extra clutch plate was fitted to trials models but one of the greatest improvements for road riders was an increase in brake diameter. While dual six-inch front brakes were retained, the single-sided rear stopper was increased from six to seven inches and a major weakness was put right.

Tappets at the base of the push rods were highly accessible behind a small cover which, because of frequent removal, was one of the reasons the bikes became known as Oily Enfields. The nickname was not always justified.

Excellent handling, with offset front fork spindles for touring models, was one of the qualities of a highly efficient design. On the debit side, the 350 Bullet weighed a pound per cubic centimetre, stand geometry called for considerable effort, and the seat height was 31 inches, a deficiency which led to the adoption of 18 inch wheels on later models.

OWNER'S STORY

Veteran still has its original paint

The bike Brian Amos rode to the 1978 TT races was the Royal Enfield 350 Bullet he bought new on May 1, 1955, for the princely sum of £201 plus £9 for panniers.

In regular use ever since, the bike has clocked 35,613 miles without major attention and is still in original paintwork and chromium plating.

A self-employed plumber, from Redhill, Surrey, Mr Amos recalls: "It is one of two Bullets a mate and I ordered in black paintwork from G Parsons and Son Motor Cycles, of Redhill.

"The bikes came with consecutive engine numbers and registration numbers. I would dearly like to locate WPL 954 of this special order. The two bikes were among the last of this type.

"Extensive frame and engine alterations were made for the Earls Court show the same year," added Mr Amos, who has won the South Eastern centre road trials championship three times with his immaculate machine.

"I generally do road trials with my wife on the back but I also have a 1960 350 Bullet in trials trim, with the front wheel spindle on the fork ends instead of offset. I ride the bike in pre-1965 trials.

"I've always found the neutral selector a handy device. It works from second, third or fourth. All you do is press it down with the heel to get neutral at traffic lights then hook the gear pedal into first.

"I know they call them Oily Enfields, but mine is fairly oil tight. I always use thick Castrol GP oil, as recommended by the makers, and I've never had any problems."

Royal Enfield Meteor Minor

In the bad old days when the Earls Court show was always in November and hardy bikers were free to ride hatless if they chose, the Royal Enfield Meteor Minor was an excellent specimen of a British 500 twin.

Outcome of a shotgun wedding between a 700 Super Meteor and a 250 Crusader, this updated version of the Redditch factory's original 500 Twin was a high performance short-stroke roadster readily identified by its small wheels.

One of the show attractions of 1958, it was actually announced in April that year, at the same time as the 700 Constellation, and remained in production without major changes for three years.

While the earlier 500 Twin, introduced in 1951, was powered by a 496cc long stroke engine (64mm x 77mm) with a claimed power output of 25bhp at 6000rpm, the Meteor Minor was the outcome of clever integration.

Sporting the same cylinders as the Super Meteor, the Meteor Minor's oversquare 496cc (70mm x 64.5mm) engine churned out some 30bhp at 6250 rpm and enabled the makers to use the same pistons for a whole range of bikes with 70mm bores.

Standardisation made it possible for the same pistons to fit 250 and 350 singles and 500 and 700 twins. This policy was extended to many other parts, notably the frame and wheels of the Crusader and Meteor Minor.

Critics who suggested that Enfield twins were little more than two cylinder versions of the firm's pre-war singles were not far off the mark! The semi-integral bottom half closely resembled that of the 350 and 500 Bullet singles and the capacity of the Meteor Minor made it, in effect, a double barrelled Crusader!

Although the power plant of the mighty 692cc Meteor, first seen in 1952, was virtually a pair of 346cc Bullet engines on a common crankcase, it is only fair to explain that the 248cc Crusader, presented to the public at the 1957 Earls Court show, was conceived and developed from scratch.

Chief designer Reg Thomas and chief engineer Tony Wilson-Jones, whose final creation was the 750 Interceptor produced until the firm folded in 1971, could never be accused of being conservative stick-in-the-muds.

At £249 10s. for a standard version with a six-inch front brake and £274 9s. for a de luxe model with seven-inch stoppers front and rear, the Meteor Minor presented good value for money.

It had light alloy con-rods with plain big-ends on a

Beefy roadster — the Meteor Minor.

massive one-piece crankshaft carried on ball and roller bearings. But the benefits of high level cams and bigger valves than the earlier 500 twin were offset by the limitations of a single Amal Monobloc carburettor.

The factory claimed that the 250 style frame and 17 inch wheels gave "an almost revolutionary degree of stability" but, in fact, the bike suffered from a lack of ground clearance. The lower seat height of 29 inches was an advantage for short riders but quick cornering yielded metallic fireworks.

A peculiar scissor clutch withdrawal mechanism was never a great success. Although tried on the bigger twins, it was eventually abandoned. The clutch thrust bearing was also prone to breaking up.

Weighing 388lb, the Meteor Minor had a top speed of 90 to 95mph. A French importer actually raced one but the earlier 500 Twin had a more impressive competition background in the International Six Days Trial.

A Six Day 500 twin on which Royal Enfield works rider Jack Stocker won a gold medal was timed at 103mph during the final speed test of the 1951 ISDT in Italy, when all the members of Britain's victorious Trophy team rode vertical twins. Those were the days!

Meteor Minor engine was the outcome of clever integration of components from other Enfields.

Specification — Royal Enfield Meteor Minor

ENGINE: Air cooled, twin cylinder, pushrod, overhead valve four stroke. Bore and stroke 70mm x 64.5mm. Capacity 496cc. Compression ratio 8 to 1. Light alloy con rods with shell big-ends. Separate cast iron barrels and alloy heads. Amal Monobloc carburettor.

TRANSMISSION: Multi-plate clutch running in oil. Duplex primary chain. Single roller rear chain. Albion four-speed gearbox bolted to engine. Overall ratios 13, 8.43, 6.06 and 4.67 to 1.

ELECTRICAL: Lucas coil ignition with 70 watt AC generator and 6 volt 12 amp hour battery. 7in. headlamp.

CAPACITIES: 3¾ gallon petrol tank, 4 pint oil tank integral with engine.

EQUIPMENT: Kickstart, dualseat, neutral selector, centre stand, tool and battery cases.

WHEELS: Steel rims with 3.25 x 17in. tyres and full width hubs.

BRAKES: 7in. diameter front and rear.

SUSPENSION: Telescopic front fork and swinging arm rear springing with three-way shocker adjustment.

DIMENSIONS: Seat height 29½in, ground clearance 6in, wheelbase 53½in, overall length 85in, weight 412lbs.

MANUFACTURERS: The Enfield Cycle Co Ltd, Redditch, Worcs.

OWNER'S STORY

Meteor makes mystery

A Welsh gardener who goes in for weight lifting in his spare time, Cedric "Little Hulk" Lloyd is the sort of chap who makes a musclebike look like a lightweight.

His 1958 Meteor Minor, which he bought from his father-in-law 17 years ago, is a bit of both. And although a growing family made Mr Lloyd switch to four wheels, he still rides the bike for pleasure.

"My father-in-law bought it new from Kings of Oxford. The total mileage is 58,000, including two trips to the Isle of Man in recent years. I have the original logbook, owners handbook — price two shillings — and pukka spares list.

"The bike is original except for the re-covering of the seat and a pattern silencer fitted when the old one lost its baffles at 11,000 miles.

"Over the years, there have been a number of internal repairs, the biggest being a rebore with new valves, guides and pistons, at 50,000 miles. I use the original pistons as polished paperweights.

"Tyres and rear chain have been replaced but the timing and distributor chains are original. The primary chain was replaced at 49,000 miles. The Lucas contact breaker points, along with the condenser and distributor cap, are still good for a few years," says Mr Lloyd, a family man from Barry, South Glamorgan.

While modern plates, rear carrier and handlebar mirror indicate that the bike is still giving yeoman service, the second owner has the original plates.

But the machine keeps its own mystery. Although it is a standard model, with optional siamesed exhaust, it has the seven inch front brake of a de luxe version. "It was bought with an incorrect five-inch brake, as fitted to the 250s of that era," he explained.

"This resulted in a visit to the Redditch factory, where a seven-inch brake was fitted for £6 in part exchange. It has been a very reliable bike but the error over the brake remains a mystery."

Scott Flying Squirrel

Now that virtually every world road racing championship class has been sewn up by watercooled two strokes, it is not inappropriate to recall that Yorkshire's temperamental Scott Flying Squirrel was the granddad of them all.

Retaining the basic features of the brainchild of Alfred Scott (1874-1923), a brilliant engineer who built disc-valve TT winners when Japan was still a hotbed of feudal aristocracy, the Scott was the vintage wonderbike that refused to die.

Never a bike for the masses, the legendary three-speeder produced until the Shipley factory folded in 1950 played as big a part in the evolution of two stroke design as the aces who immortalised the Scott trial as a major sporting classic.

It was a unique if somewhat perverse machine which could send owners into ecstasies or drive them up the wall. It had a very special kind of charisma which, to the hard-bitten enthusiast, made it the very best of British.

More expensive and infinitely more fickle than most of its four stroke contemporaries, the last of a remarkable line had a rigid back end, Dowty air forks modified to spring suspension, and other postwar innovations.

Dowty forks, also fitted by the manufacturers of Panther and Velocette, were slimmer than most teles of the period. They worked admirably but eventual leakages from inflation valves and worn seals prompted the conversion to oil-damped coils.

Suitable for solo or sidecar work, the Flying Squirrel sported a fully triangulated duplex frame, straight tubes forming an extremely strong and torsionally rigid structure with a low centre of gravity for the motor.

Squatting below a distinctive radiator with a cylindrical header tank, the 596cc engine (73mm x 71.4mm bore and stroke) was a replica of a long-forgotten TT racer, the first touring Flying Squirrels being produced in 1927.

Over the years, the engine retained a separate alloy head and distinctive cylinders painted red. It was a three-port stroker, with a downdraught carburettor, but the most traditional feature was a massive nine-inch flywheel in the middle of a 180 degree crankshaft. Spinning in the fresh air between the two crankcase compression chambers, this flywheel was the key to central chain primary drive to a gearbox famed for its massive pedal (one up and two down) and unmistakable clutch plate rattle when the clutch was withdrawn.

Scott's Flying Squirrel was the pioneer of today's racing two strokes. This is a 1950 model.

An example of the 'new' vintage Scott that Mike Berry, car and bike restoration specialist from South West London, planned to produce in 1971. Lack of components brought the scheme to a halt.

Specification — Scott Flying Squirrel

ENGINE: Watercooled, twin cylinder, two stroke. Bore and stroke 73mm x 71.4mm. Capacity 596cc. Compression ratio 6.5 to 1. Detachable alloy head. Cooling by thermo syphon radiator. Amal carburettor.

TRANSMISSION: Multi-plate clutch. Single row central primary chain and left-hand secondary chain. Three-speed footchange gearbox. Overall ratios (close) 8.90, 5.50 and 4.18 to 1.

ELECTRICS: Lucas coil ignition with 70 watt dynamo and 6 volt 13 amp hour battery. 7in. headlamp.

CAPACITIES: 4 gallons petrol, ½ gallon oil (total loss pump).

EQUIPMENT: Kickstarter, spring saddle, twin tool boxes, rear stand.

WHEELS: Steel rims, transmission shock absorber in rear hub. Tyres 3.00 x 19in. front, 3.25 x 19in. rear.

SUSPENSION: Dowty pneumatic front fork with oil damping. Rigid back end.

DIMENSIONS: Seat height 29½in, ground clearance 5in, wheelbase 57in, overall length 86in, weight 362lbs.

MANUFACTURERS: The Scott Motor Cycle Co, Shipley, Yorkshire.

Coil ignition eliminated the long magneto chain of earlier models, making room for a five-pint oil tank to feed the total loss Pilgrim oil pump which was undoubtedly the bike's own worst enemy. Driven off the offside crank, which also carried a skew gear for a car-type distributor, the duplex pump was difficult to adjust and unpredictable in operation.

A well at the base of each crank chamber was a get-you-home provision for riders whose oil supply failed or dried up, but agitation on bumpy roads often raised a smoke screen.

OWNER'S STORY

Easily keeps up with modern traffic

One of the last examples to leave the Yorkshire factory, the 1950 Scott Flying Squirrel owned by John Lycett, chief engineer with a dumper manufacturing company, is a far cry from the bikes he rode as an apprentice in the Midlands.

"When I had to motor cycle I always viewed a Scott with awe. I could never afford one in those days but I admired them as something very special," he recalled at his home in Warwick where the Scott is the companion of a Citroen, a Vincent Comet and a Cyclemaster of the early fifties!

"I bought the Scott in 1974. I was toying with the idea of treating myself to a 700 ES Silk Scott and George Silk put me on to it. It was a well kept specimen but the owner, who lived in London, had to give up riding because of ill health.

"It was originally fitted with a wide ratio gearbox, available as an optional extra, and was converted to close ratios shortly before I bought it, giving 4.18, 5.50 and 8.90 instead of 4.18, 6.08 and 12.1 to 1.

"As it pulls a rather high gear, the engine needs plenty of revs to get going. I've not taken it over 70 mph but it will easily keep up with modern traffic and I've never had an involuntary stop.

"Vibration is never more than a tingle and I keep the oil pump setting a bit rich rather than risk nipping up the engine. It is much happier on a long run through the Cotswolds than on short journeys.

"The bike is a bit of a menace in town traffic. It ticks over nicely but engulfs everybody in smoke

A pancake Lucas six-volt 70 watt dynamo, driven from the nearside crank and bolted to the crank case door, replaced the old magdyno. The ignition system included automatic advance and retard but the carburettor, which acquired a good air cleaner, retained a manual air lever.

As unconventional as the rest of the bike, the petrol tank held three-and-a-half gallons. Other good features were a slick gear change and a roll-on centre stand which required the minimum of effort.

Wider mudguards with stronger stays and a bigger headlamp were detail improvements on the 1950 models displayed at the 1949 Earls Court show. The machines had dual front brakes but, at £252 11d, including the dreaded UK purchase tax, a Scott was a luxury few could afford.

Although Scott owners like to refer to the inimitable yowl of their siamesed exhausts, only the racing versions of these comparatively slow-revving two strokes were really musical. The road bike, which had a claimed power output of 30bhp at 5000 rpm and a top speed of about 80mph, was a well behaved thoroughbred with smooth acceleration and tireless performance.

when you pull away. I suppose it is a bit anti-social in that respect!

"I haven't done any really long journeys but I think it handles well. You have to stand up for riding over pot holes but, despite the rigid end, it isn't bad. If you consider that it is really a 1930 model with telescopic forks, then it's a tremendous bike."

Mr Lycett, a vintage enthusiast, whose first bike was a 1927 225cc Royal Enfield two stroke with an outside flywheel — "I wish I had it now" — has good reason to be proud of his fine specimen. It's engine number is DPY 5423. The last to leave the Shipley factory was DPY 5426. The prefix denotes the detachable head.

Sunbeam S7

When the Sunbeam S7 made its first appearance over 30 years ago the road testers of the most esteemed magazine of the day told their readers they felt unable to produce a road test of the machine after riding it "just 1,000 miles".

It was, they said, just too new and different — the test would have to take twice as many miles as usual.

To the motor cyclists of the time the S7 was so different as to be hailed, even then, in 1946, as far ahead of its time. Looking at the bike now you have to agree that it is a remarkable achievement in the history of the motor cycle.

A measure of the degree of innovation is apparent when you hear that Sunbeam applied for no fewer than 30 patents when the S7 appeared.

Just look at the engine alone and you'll see why the S7 immediately springs to mind whenever anyone mentions the name of Sunbeam.

What could have been more different than an overhead cam, over square, in-line twin with all-alloy block and crankcase in one casting with wet sump lubrication, car-type clutch and shaft drive, to say nothing of coil ignition and a rubber mounted engine?

The S7 featured massive tyres — 4.50 x 16 front and 4.75 x 16 rear — when most bikes were still using 3.25 x 19 covers. Also in an age when most manufacturers seemed to cling to the tenet that spartan seating was the thing, Sunbeam came up with an amazing cantilever suspension system for the saddle, which allied to the rear plunger and front telescopic forks that replaced the prototype model's sliders with central damper gave a really smooth ride.

The S7 was designed by Erling Poppe, a man who had previously worked in the auto and bus industries and it was he who brought the very 'car-like' qualities to the machine.

The first 100 Sunbeam S7s saw the light of day in late 1946 and were shipped to Africa. However they were recalled after complaints of serious vibration. It was then that Poppe and his team came up with the rubber mounts — at the front and back of the head and under the gearbox.

The over square cylinder arrangement — 70 x 63.5 mm was chosen to reduce piston speed and help to make the alloy unit a little quieter. Short stubby finning on both block and crankcase also helped in this respect by reducing resonance.

This S7 first saw the light of day in 1950 and the model was to continue in one guise or another for six years. Note the saddle which is cantilever sprung with a damper inside the frame tubes.

Surprisingly, noise was one of the main reasons for adopting the overhead cam system, that and the fact that the firm had settled on the in-line layout and wanted it as narrow as possible.

Neatness was another innovation which baffled the public when the S7 appeared. Until then few designers had paid any attention to the theory that things should be as uncluttered as possible. With the wet sump system employed the machine needed no external oil pipes and in fact nothing clutters the clean lines of the motor. Even the plugs are concealed behind a finned cover to preserve the lines.

The front of the engine is the only place to reveal an unsightly bulge and that's just the dynamo which is mounted on the end of the single throw, one piece crankshaft. At the rear of the head, only the distributor extends.

A six volt battery is concealed behind a cover on one side — again very unusual for its day — and the corresponding cover on the other side hides the wiring. Tools are concealed in a small box low down on the right side.

Forward thinking even extended to the kickstart which was twisted through 90 degrees by employing bevel gears to enable it to operate in the conventional direction. Final drive was by underslung worm and wheel drive through a shaft which was exposed to the elements.

In 1949 the firm produced a Deluxe version of the S7 which featured a compression ratio upped from 6.5 to 6.8 and a cast aluminium silencer instead of a steel item. The same year also saw the introduction of the sporty version of the bike — the S8 which had a compression ratio of 7.2:1 and was considerably slimmer and trimmer.

The fat tyres were the first to go and in came more conventional 3.25 x 19 and 3.50 x 18 covers along with a 7 inch BSA type front brake which featured conventional adjustment as opposed to the car type adjusters on the S7. Sunbeam also opted for BSA forks on the sportier (and cheaper) S8. The seat was the conventional saddle with two chrome springs at the rear.

OWNER'S STORY

A dream built from a garden heap

When lorry driver David Gardner was using motor cycles as a primary form of transport it was his ambition to own a Sunbeam S7.

But in those days the 'beam was one of the three most expensive machines on the market so David was unable to realise his dream. It wasn't until many years later, that he became the proud owner of his first S7.

The machine was in a heap in a garden in Oldham. He piled the pieces in the back of his A40 van and carted them home to Great Horwood, Bucks, and then discovered he had a 1950 S7 De Luxe.

It took David about a year of working practically every night and most weekends to get the bike into its original showroom condition and since then he has covered several thousand miles on the machine, including a trip to the 1977 TT.

The second of David's bikes — a 1952 S8 — was in a pretty sorry state when he bought it from Stewart Engineering in Putney, the only firm which still makes Sunbeam spares. Again a year of evenings and weekends put things right and helped the machine take the best S8 award at the annual Sunbeam club rally.

Latest project was a brace of very early S7s with frame numbers 310 and 539, some of the earliest still in captivity. Parts are very difficult to come by and he has had to make the inverted handlebar levers himself.

The only slight modification he has allowed is the addition of mirrors and a windscreen to the S7 and a mirror to the S8.

Beautifully engineered, the Sunbeam S7 was the subject of no less than 30 patents when it appeared over 30 years ago.

Specification — Sunbeam S7

ENGINE: Air cooled, in-line, twin-cylinder, overhead camshaft four-stroke. Bore and stroke 70mm x 63.5mm. Capacity 487cc. Compression ratio 6.5 to 1. Alloy cylinder block and head. Amal carburettor.

TRANSMISSION: Seven-inch, single plate, car-type clutch splined to four-speed gearbox mainshaft. Foot change box in unit with engine. Shaft drive via bevels in rear hub. Overall ratios: 14.5, 9.0, 6.5 and 5.3 to 1.

ELECTRICAL: Lucas coil ignition with 60 watt dynamo and 6 volt, 12 amp hour battery. Auto advance and retard in distributor, 8in. headlamp.

EQUIPMENT: Kickstart, hinge and plunger saddle, tool and battery cases, rubber engine mountings, prop and centre stands.

CAPACITIES: 3½ gallon petrol tank, 4 pint oil reservoir.

WHEELS: Interchangeable front and rear. Steel rims with 16in. x 4.50 and/or 4.75 tyres.

BRAKES: 8in. drums front and rear.

SUSPENSION: Telescopic front fork and plunger rear springing with hydraulic damping.

DIMENSIONS: Seat height 30in, ground clearance 4½in, wheelbase 57in, overall length 87in, weight 432lbs.

MANUFACTURERS: BSA Motor Cycles Ltd (Sunbeam Division), Small Heath, Birmingham 11.

Triumph TR5

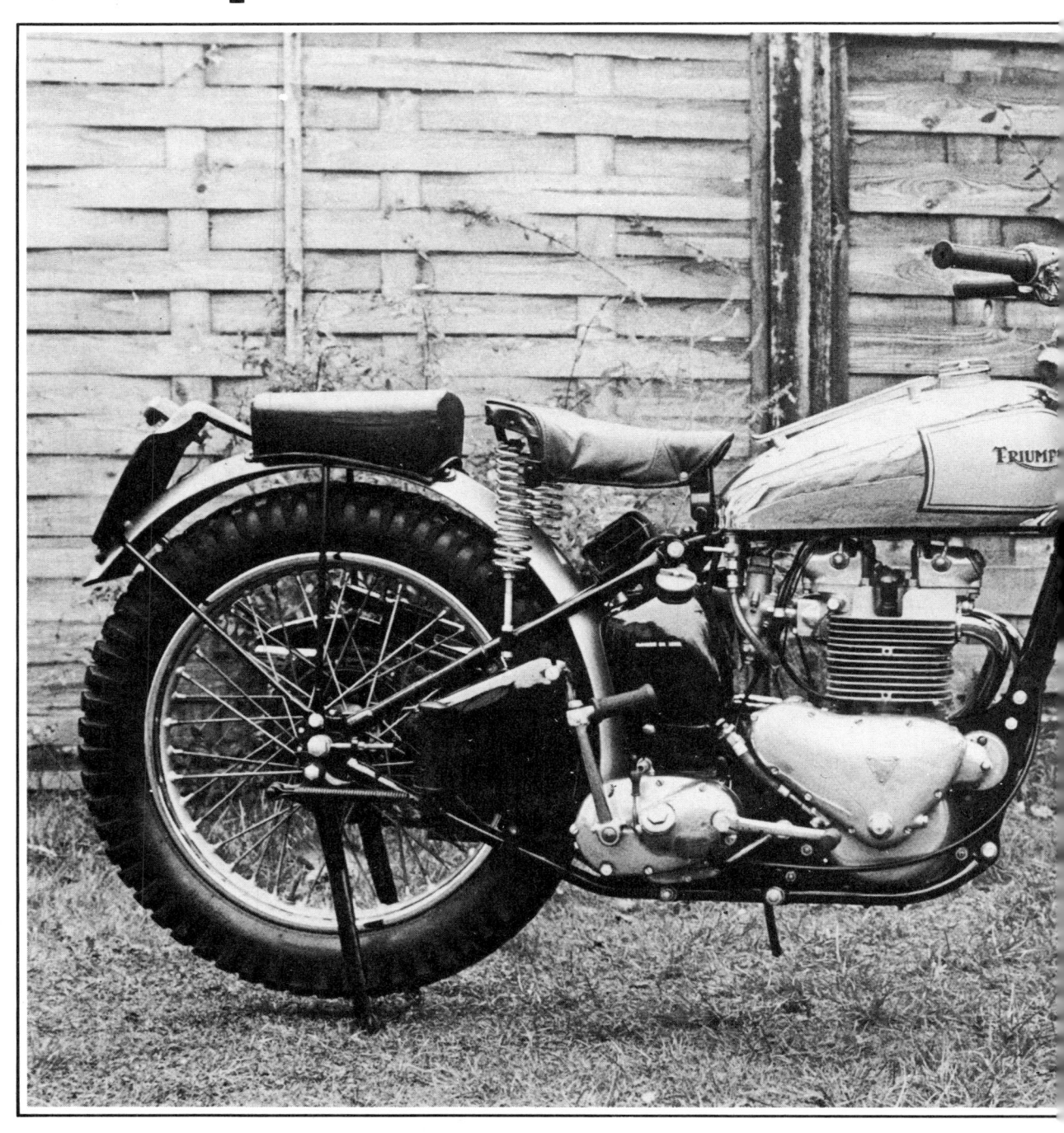

The 500cc Triumph TR5 made a big impact in the world of International Six Day Trials during the post-war years, and with its sister machine, the GP, made a two pronged attack on the sporting field both on and off the road.

Both the Grand Prix and the TR5 first appeared in production in 1948, both with basically the same "generator" engines. These engines had been built during the war to power mobile generators used by the RAF.

After the war, the generator style cylinder head and barrels — distinctive because of the square shaped fins — were the only castings available, so they were used for the motor cycle engines.

The barrels and heads were square shaped to fit neatly into the generator pack, and the barrels feature attachment points for the cowling. These

Specification — Triumph TR5

ENGINE: All alloy air cooled, twin cylinder, push rod overhead valve four stroke. Bore and stroke 63mm x 80mm. Capacity 498cc. Compression ratio 6 to 1. Plain big end bearings. Amal carburettor.

TRANSMISSION: Multi-plate clutch in oil. Four-speed footchange gearbox. Overall ratios 11.66, 8.44, 5.69 and 4.8 to 1. Single roller primary and secondary chains.

ELECTRICAL: Magneto ignition, separate dynamo, 6 volt 13 amp hour battery.

CAPACITIES: 2½ gallons petrol, 6 pints oil.

EQUIPMENT: Kickstarter, tank top grill, front and centre stands, pillion pad.

WHEELS: Steel rims with 3.00 x 20in front tyre, 4.00 x 19in rear. Fabricated hubs.

BRAKES: 7in. diameter drums front and rear.

SUSPENSION: Rigid rear with telescopic front forks.

DIMENSIONS: Wheelbase 52in, ground clearance 5½in, dry weight 295lbs.

MANUFACTURER: Triumph Engineering Co Ltd, Meriden Works, Allesley, Coventry.

It took about three and a half years to gather all the correct equipment for this 1949 TR5

engines were the first all-alloy motors made by Triumph and the heads also featured parallel exhaust ports.

The TR5 was developed specially for the ISDTs, because the current Speed Twins were too low to the ground. Other improvements were lighter weight (about 320lb) and a new, shorter wheelbase rigid frame.

ISDT successes were scored at the hands of British team captain Alan Jefferies and team members Jim Alves and Bert Gaymer. The ISDT manufacturers team prize was taken by Triumph every year between 1948 and 1951.

The TR5 could have formed the basis for the Army machine of the time — but the Army insisted on a side-valve engine, so the TRW was born, using the TR5 frame.

The square barrel and head style was dropped from 1952 when the model used a Tiger 100 top end with fine pitched finning. A swinging arm frame was introduced in 1955.

The Grand Prix machine, which enjoyed a Manx GP win ridden by Ernie Lyons in 1946, had the frame of a Tiger and although the engine was externally similar, internals gave the engine a higher state of tune. During that 1946 GP, Lyons set the fastest lap at nearly 79mph.

The GP was produced in small numbers — only some 150 were made — but they proved popular with clubmen.

First all-alloy motor to be made by Triumph, the TR5 also featured parallel exhaust ports.

OWNER'S STORY

Ideal dual purpose bike

An immaculate 1949 Triumph TR5, restored to virtually standard condition, is thought to be worth a four-figure sum, such is its rarity. One proud owner is Dave Naylor, of Sutton, Surrey. He bought his machine in 1974 for £300. Since then he has searched for original parts — such as head and barrel, petrol tank and numerous small items such as the tail light. He was careful to get the right throttle, carburettor rubbers, kickstart and three-bar tank grid.

The bike is now in "works" spec and good for 80mph on the road — attainable because of wide ratios in the gearbox.

"My bike is now too immaculate to be used in trials," said Mr Naylor, "but in its day it was the ideal dual purpose bike. I like the machine because it is easy to work on and looks nice — but it is the sort of thing you either like or don't like. In earlier days you would not have caught me on one."

Riding the bike, with its rigid frame and sprung saddle gives a reasonably comfortable journey, said Mr Naylor, but it is in no way comparable to a modern machine.

He is keen to trace the owner or owners of the machine between 1949 and 1955, and would be interested to hear if the machine has a competition history. It was first sold in Birmingham with the registration number KOC 532. His address is 23 Kingsley Avenue, Sutton, Surrey.

Mr Naylor also has a 1955 TR5 for four stroke trials and green lane riding, with a large rear wheel sprocket and BSA C11 pistons, giving about four to one compression.

As chairman of Croydon MCC, he organises green lane runs and other biking activities. For work he alternates between an XS750 Yamaha, a 1960 BMW R50 and a 1974 TR5T.

Triumph Tiger 100A

Never a full-blooded Tiger 100, but a mild-mannered 500 which inherited the cobby styling of the 350 Triumph Twenty One, the T100A appeared at a time when motor cycling was still struggling to shake off the grimy grease-monkey image.

Edward Turner, the autocratic supremo of the Meriden factory responsible for many brilliant designs, firmly believed that road riders wanted to be clean, dry, quiet and tidy when, in fact, the majority wanted to look racers.

Slower than the original Tiger 100, with close pitched alloy cylinder fins and separate gearbox, the unit construction T100A was really a sheep in wolf's clothing and it remained in production only two years.

Introduced in 1960 and improved for 1961, it was the forerunner of the more fiery T100SS, T100C, T100R Daytona and Trophy 500 models. All too often, second-hand bikes were cannibalised and the engines grafted into scramblers.

The distinctive "bathtub" back end and deeply valanced front mudguard first appeared on the 3TA, the highly successful Twenty One launched in 1957 to commemorate Triumph's 21 years of motor cycle production.

The 3TA was one of the most trouble-free bikes ever built and its Twenty One name tag had a clever double meaning. In American biking jargon, a 350 is more frequently described as a 21 cubic incher.

In 1959, the 5TA Speed Twin was given the "bathtub" treatment influenced by the scooter boom of the period. In 1960, the styling was extended to the T100A, with energy transfer ignition, high compression pistons and special camshafts.

The price was £247 15s 10d including the pillion pegs, propstand and other bits of kit which, in those days, were cunningly listed as optional extras. The price included the dreaded Purchase Tax, a more discriminating imposition than today's VAT.

But the new Lucas ignition proved troublesome. A return to conventional coil ignition was the most notable improvement for 1961. While the change meant going back to a battery, it ensured more reliable sparking than the ingenious but fickle energy transfer system.

A bigger Amal Monobloc carburettor (1 inch instead of 7/8 inch) and more efficient camshaft helped to raise the claimed power output from 32 to 34bhp at 7,000rpm.

An elegant touring bike, the unit construction Triumph Tiger 100A of 1960 and 1961 was a comparatively tame version of a lively species. This rebuild is probably one of the finest in existence.

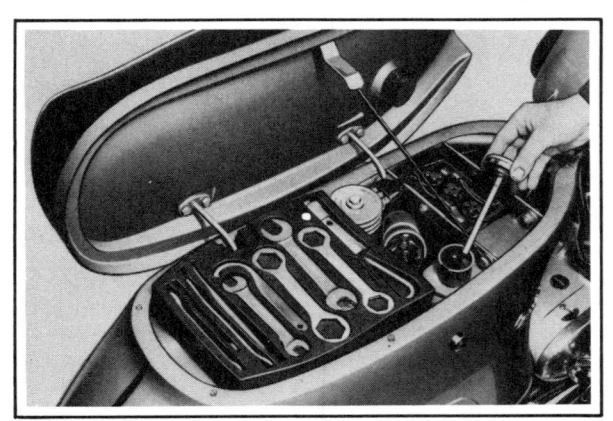

Like the Triumph Twenty-One, tools were neatly presented beneath a hinged dualseat.

Specification — Triumph Tiger 100A

ENGINE: Air cooled, twin cylinder, overhead valve, pushrod four stroke. Bore and stroke 69mm x 65.5mm. Capacity 490cc. Compression ratio 9.0 to 1. Cast iron barrel and aluminium alloy head. Amal Monobloc carburettor.

TRANSMISSION: Multi-plate clutch in oil. Duplex primary and final chain. Integral footchange gearbox. Overall ratios 11.6, 8.4, 5.7 and 4.8 to 1.

ELECTRICS: Lucas RM 15 alternator with energy transfer (later reverted to coil ignition). 6 volt 12 amp hour battery. 7in. headlamp.

CAPACITIES: 3½ gallons petrol, 5 pints oil.

EQUIPMENT: Folding kickstarter, tank luggage grid, dualseat, centre roll-on stand, tyre pump, steering damper, tool kit carried under seat in moulded rubber tray. Side stand and pillion rests available as extras.

WHEELS: Steel rims. Tyres 3.25 x 17in ribbed front, 3.50 x 17in studded rear.

BRAKES: 7in. drums front and rear.

SUSPENSION: Telescopic spring forks with two-way hydraulic damping, Girling oil-damped shock absorbers.

DIMENSIONS: Seat height 28½in, ground clearance 5in, wheelbase 51¾in, overall length 80in, weight 374lbs.

MANUFACTURERS: Triumph Engineering Co Ltd, Meriden Works, Allesley, Warwickshire.

The only other change was cosmetic, with black and silver paintwork instead of the earlier black and ivory which distinguished the so-called sports version from the traditional burgundy of the softer Speed Twin.

The T100A retained 490cc engine dimensions (69mm x 65.5mm bore and stroke) with a cast iron cylinder block painted silver to match the aluminium

OWNER'S STORY

Authentic down to the last nut and bolt

After two years of painstaking restoration, during which he searched the length and breadth of Britain for genuine Triumph parts. Terry Hume completed his 1961 Tiger to "as new" condition.

Authentic down to the last nut and bolt, the bike is now a potential concours winner, yet Mr Hume, an electronics engineer from Buntingford, Herts., bought it as a rusty heap in 1976.

"It had 35,000 miles on the clock and was completely clapped out. I gave £85 for a mass of oil leaks, burnt exhaust valves, chains stretched to destruction, and loads of play in all the bushes.

"I had a 1960 T100A when I lived in Edmonton. It was the last bike I owned before I got married and started a family so rebuilding this one was really a nostalgic exercise.

"A spares list proved invaluable — if I had not been able to quote part numbers I am sure Triumph dealers would not have located all the obsolete bits I needed.

"Locating pressed steel rear panels proved a major problem. The pressings for 350s and 500s were half an inch shorter than those for 650s and the fixings were different.

"In the end, I got a right-hand panel from Edinburgh and a left-hand panel from Swansea. One was from a blue 3TA, the other from a red 5TA. The whole job cost me about £600.

"I rebuilt the wheels with genuine Dunlop/Triumph numbered rims, which took longer to find than a pair of pukka silencers under a pile of pattern components.

"The engine vibrates a fair bit. It has a critical period at around 55 to 60mph but I have never taken it over 80mph," says Mr Hume.

alloy head. Compression ratio was 9 to 1. Valve gear was a little more noisy than the cooking version.

With the physical dimensions of a 350, the T100A was an attractive proposition for smaller riders. Luxurious details included the famous Triumph headlamp nacelle, tank luggage grid and a foam rubber moulding under the seat for a laid-out toolkit.

Superb but extremely vulnerable mudguards gave the bike a slick appearance but it was never a howling success. Engine and frame numbers started at H22430 and finished at H25251.

In the end, the Triumph Tiger 100 was stripped of its trimmings. Doug Hele, the engineer in charge of development, came up with the twin-carburettor Daytona version capable of 125mph. And Triumph customers got what they always wanted.

Triumph Tiger 110

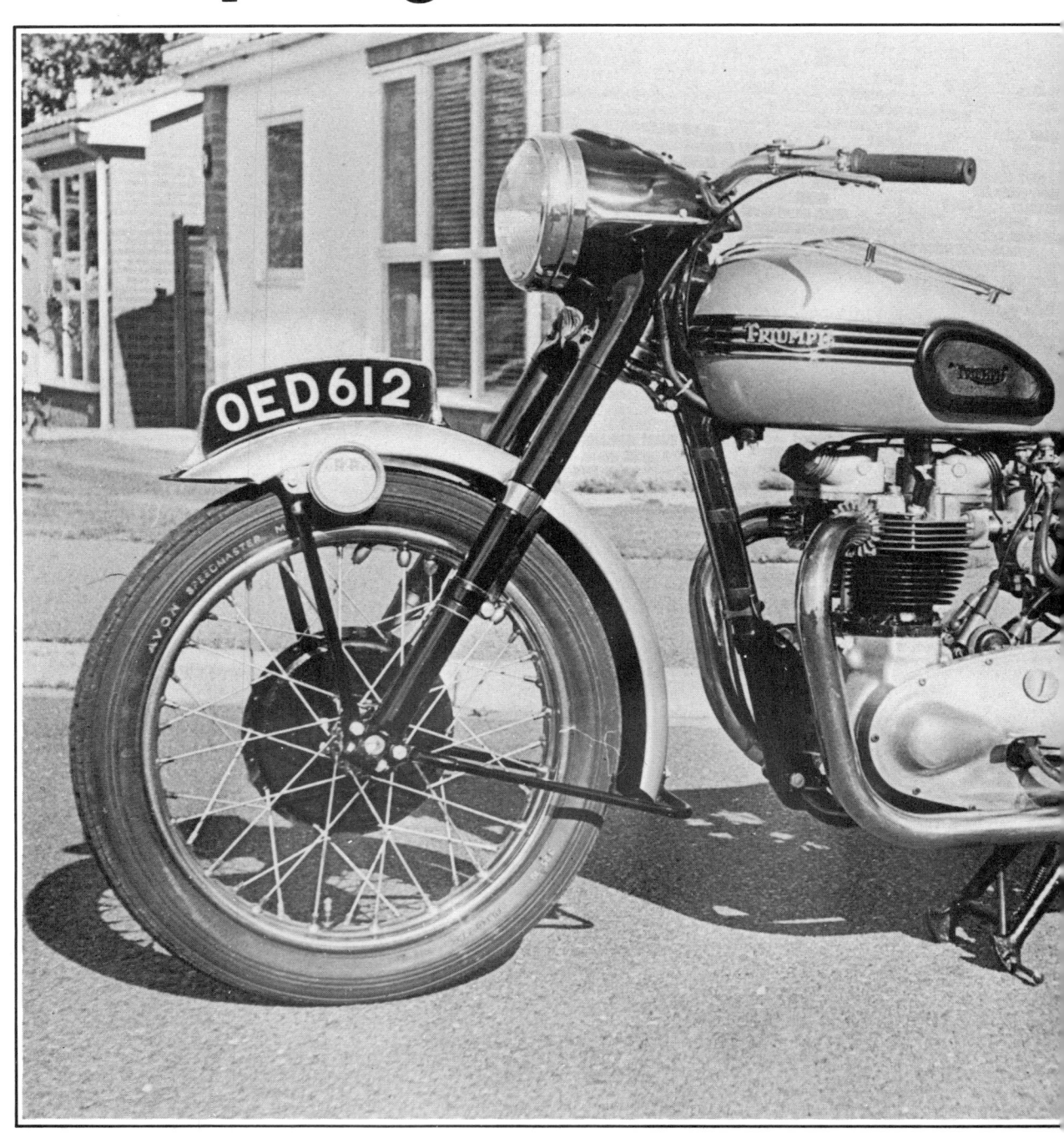

Ton-up version of the 650 Thunderbird, the Triumph Tiger 110 was originally introduced for the American market when budding world champion Kenny Roberts was a toddler and annual road tax in the UK was still under four quid!

It was an attractive and successful dollar earner which fulfilled an insatiable demand from the world's biggest bike consumers for the highest possible output from Triumph's biggest-twin.

First launched in 1954, with swinging arm rear suspension instead of Triumph's ingenious but virtually ineffective sprung hub, the T110 retained a cast iron cylinder head until 1956 when improvements included a redesigned light-alloy head. A more tidy appearance was achieved by using the pushrod tubes for valve gear oil drainage, instead of external pipes, while cooling was considerably improved by slotting air passages into the alloy casting.

In 1956, the T110's performance was second only to that of 1000cc Vincents of the period. It would cruise at 80mph on half-throttle (no 70 limit in those days), could be hammered at 90 without complaining, and would just about reach 110mph with a tailwind.

While vibration was not entirely non-existent, and steering sometimes became light-hearted when the full potential was exploited by an enthusiastic right hand, the bike was quick enough to satisfy the most discerning road burners.

An air filter neatly sandwiched between the six-pint oil tank and the six-volt battery box did not appreciably restrict the performance of an engine which, despite 8.5 to 1 compression pistons, was remarkably economical. Throttle-happy valve bouncers could trigger off a dramatic thirst by rasping up to 75mph in second, and so on, but it was not necessary to dawdle to get more than 70mpg from the single Amal Monobloc carburettor.

The position of the air lever, almost inaccessibly tucked under the seat, reflected the passion for tidiness of Triumph supremo Edward Turner and his trusty team. It was the perfect place to fumble with thick gloves on a cold day! Obviously put there for the benefit of Californians who never used it, the air lever was useful for starting in cooler climates. Firing up was helped by half retarding the magneto ignition lever which, mercifully, remained on the handlebars.

Not unlike recent Meriden twins, this restored 1956 Tiger 110 with separate engine/gearbox and big, alloy primary case is now comparitively rare. Rocker box caps and silencers are not original.

Designed when nearly all British speed cops were Triumph mounted, and bike hi-jackers almost invariably got caught, the T110 was devoid of ignition keys and steering locks but was fitted with a cut-out button in the headlamp nacelle.

An ammeter in the stylish nacelle was a frequent victim of vibration. And while substantial taper petrol taps were stiff enough to be unaffected by the tingles, gripping the four-gallon tank between the knees at any speed over 80 resulted in the perfect vibro-massage. The rider's half of the dual seat was one of the most comfortable in the business. The pillion part was equally generous but the width between the passenger's thighs was not to every maiden's liking.

The eight-inch front brake, with a ribbed drum and ventilated air scoop, was super-efficient. It was most effective at high speeds and easily made the front tyre squeal. Along with other Triumphs of the same era, part of the front brake inner cable ran through a stiff outer casing parallel with the fork leg.

Then the only British manufacturer with a down-for-down gearshift, Triumph had a few problems with oil seeping from the mainshaft of the separate four-speed box but cog selection was always good.

Although items like a quickly detachable back wheel, pillion footrests and prop stand were optional extras, the smart shell-blue and black finish of the Tiger 110 concealed a truly feline character. Depending on how it was ridden, it would purr like a kitten or snarl like a predator. Not surprisingly, it was the forerunner of the more powerful twin-carb Bonneville.

Overshadowed only by 1000cc Vincents at the time, the Tiger 110 motor would tolerate rasps up to 75mph in second.

Specification — Triumph Tiger 110

ENGINE: Air cooled, twin cylinder, pushrod, overhead valve four stroke. Bore and stroke 71mm x 82mm. Capacity 649cc. Compression ratio 8.5 to 1. Cast iron cylinder block. Alloy head, light alloy con rods, plain big-ends, Amal Monobloc carburettor.

TRANSMISSION: Multi-plate clutch in oil bath. Single roller primary and rear chains. Four-speed footchange gearbox. Overall ratios: 11.2, 7.75, 5.45 and 4.57 to 1.

ELECTRICAL: Lucas magneto ignition with manual advance/retard. Separate 60 watt dynamo and 6 volt battery for lights. 7in. headlamp.

CAPACITIES: 4 gallon petrol tank, 6 pint oil tank.

EQUIPMENT: Kickstarter, prop and centre stands, duel seat, tank top parcel carrier.

WHEELS: Steel rims with 3.25 x 19in. ribbed front and 3.50 x 19in. studded rear tyre.

BRAKES: 8in. front drum with ventilating scoop, 7in. rear. Finger adjusters.

SUSPENSION: Triumph telescopic fork with hydraulic damping and swinging arm rear springing with three-way shockers.

DIMENSIONS: Seat height 31in, ground clearance 5in, wheelbase 57in, overall length 86in, weight 390lbs.

MANUFACTURERS: Triumph Engineering Co Ltd. Meriden Works, Allesley, Coventry, Warwickshire.

OWNER'S STORY

Memento of a vintage year for British bikes

A supermarket operator who was once an AA patrolman with a BSA M21 box sidecar outfit on the Bonnie Banks of Loch Lomond, Ian Pettigrew spent nearly four years restoring the 1956 Tiger 110 he literally saved from the scrap heap.

"It was in a terrible state when I bought it. Riding it back from Southport was one of the most hair-raising experiences of my life," recalled the Scot from Glasgow who now lives in Lytham St Annes, Lancs. The bike had been painted red, the engine spewed oil and rattled horribly, and the front brake had packed up. It was an absolute death trap and the previous owner had become afraid of it.

"I wanted this particular machine as I regard 1956 as a vintage year for the British industry. It was a time when they had debugged some of their best designs and had not yet become obsessed with fancy ideas like bathtub back ends.

"I had the engine rebuilt by a Triumph specialist. It is the original engine, with the same number as the frame which I took to Manchester to be enamelled. The rest I did myself, including re-covering the seat.

"I learned a lot from rebuilding a Sunbeam S7 of the same year. I got a pair of new mudguards from a firm in Stoke on Trent and various bits and pieces from advertisements. I sprayed the tank myself, made one ammeter from a pair of old ones, obtained new fork shrouds because the originals had been sawn down, and advertised for a rider's handbook before I got one from a neighbour in the next street!

"My aim has been to restore the bike back to original without spivving it up to concours standards."

Triumph Tiger Cub

Triumph Tiger Cub T20 as it appeared in November, 1961, with top speed approaching 80mph. Above right: Dresse

...ual gear, the Sports Cub (T20S/S) of similar vintage.

Triumph's Tiger Cub set new standards of performance in the lightweight bike field during the early 1960s.

The company had built nothing but twin cylinder machines from the end of the war until the 149cc Terrier made its debut in 1953, and it was the following year that the 199cc Cub appeared.

A bigger bore was the main difference between the two machines, but the Cub went on to gain 16in. wheels, and later a swinging arm. Development on the bike produced roadster, sports, trials and scrambles versions of the basic machine.

Near 80mph speeds were attainable on the 1961 T20S/L cub. At £165, this little machine set standards for the class. It was a road going version of the scrambles machine which was exported to the United States. The 'L' indicated it had a lighting conversion from coils in the energy transfer ignition system.

Standard machines had 7 to 1 compression ratios, but the sports bike had 9 to 1 and a high lift cam. Another sporting feature was the ISDT style air filter. Suspension, based on units used on larger machines, gave the bike a firm, sporting, ride.

The standard low compression Cub's performance was lively by the standards of the day, with a top speed of about 70mph and nippy acceleration. Economy was a big feature and average consumption of about 100mpg could be expected.

In 1964 Triumph offered only three Cub models, the T20 roadster, with lightweight fork and headlamp nacelle, the T20 SH Sports Cub and the TR20 Trials Cub. The scrambler was dropped because there was no demand for a 200cc machine.

The T20 roadster then cost £170, the sportster £188 and the trials bike £200. Cheaper still were Triumph's two scooters, the 100cc Tina and 175cc Tigress.

After a production run of about 12 years, which saw many detail and model changes, the Cub was phased out in favour of the 250cc machines.

Velocette Vogue

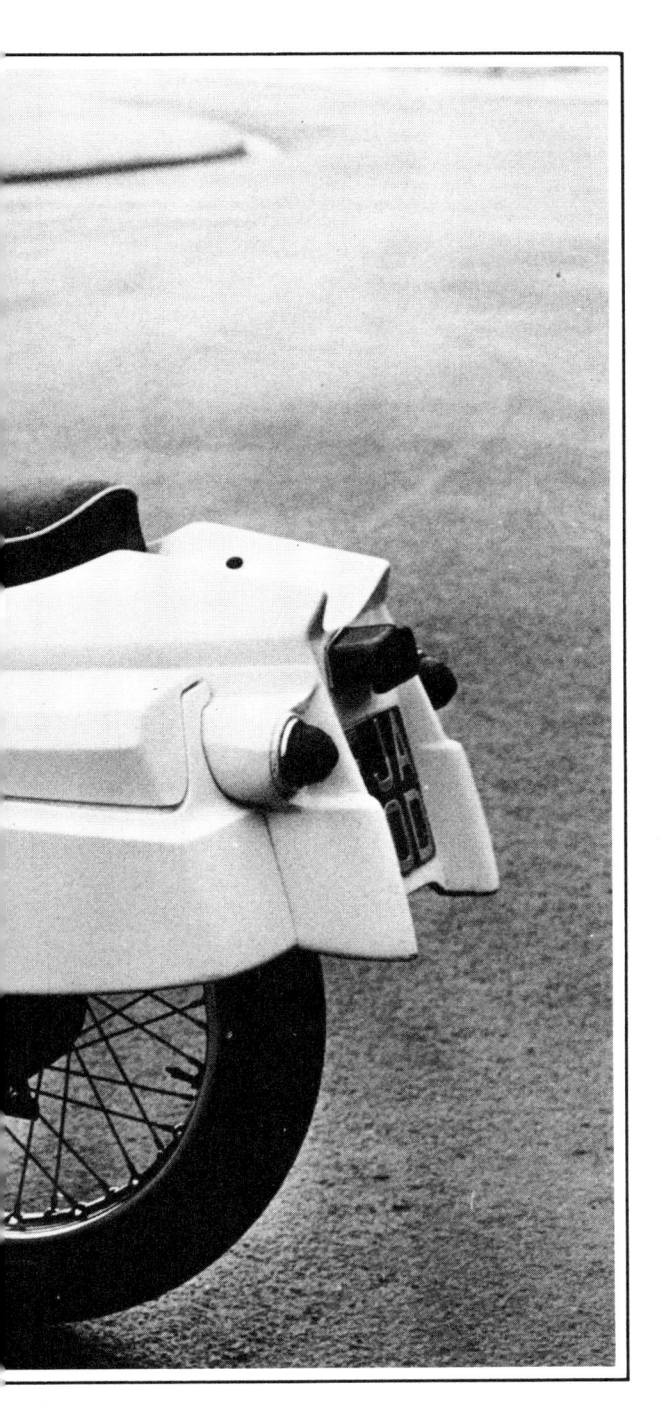

A luxurious all-weather runabout, the glass-fibre bodied Velocette Vogue was one of the most glorious commercial fiascos the British industry ever dreamed up.

Underpowered for serious touring, it was nevertheless a delightful little bike which handled so well that it was virtually undroppable.

It was smooth, silent and safe. It was rust-proofed, economical and easy to clean. It was futuristic and practically fool-proof yet, unlike the ubiquitous LE, the Vogue never really caught on.

Only 381 were produced by the Hall Green, Birmingham, factory, between February 1963, when it was launched, and September 1968, when it was dropped.

With built-in legshields, glove boxes, footboards and panniers, originally extras but later thrown in, the two-tone (cream/beige or cream/blue) glass-fibre matched the superb engineering underneath. The Mitchenall-designed body was really solid. The moulds have long vanished but the material was a quarter-of-an-inch thick in places. Experts reckon such mouldings would cost nearly £500 to make today.

Weak points included an integral petrol tank and an unsupported Perspex windscreen so tall that it invariably cracked under the strain of being buffeted at speeds of up to 60mph.

Twin headlamps and flashers, operated by a simple dashboard switch, were good features, as were quickly detachable side panels for engine maintenance and a hinged seat with recesses underneath for toolkit and battery. But stripping the bike down to its chassis took about four hours.

Power unit and shaft-drive transmission were similar to the LE Mark III, with minor modifications to the 192cc (50mm x 49mm) bore and stroke **watercooled side valve flat twin engine, but the** chassis was very different.

Unlike the "Noddy Bike", which sported a pressed steel chassis, the Vogue enjoyed a tubular frame with a massive 2½ diameter spine from the steering head. Only the box-section front down tube and radiator were similar to the LE.

With hefty body brackets and a sub-frame to support the glass-fibre tail, the Vogue weighed 275lbs. This was 25lbs heavier than the LE Mark III and the performance suffered accordingly.

Originally fitted with six-volt Miller electrics, the

A sawn-off screen and choke toggle glued to the tickler of the carburettor (below tank badge) are the only non-standard items on this 1966 Velocette Vogue. Note stepped footrests for rider and passenger.

bike acquired 12 volt Lucas equipment in January 1966, involving a different flywheel generator and other bits and pieces.

Twin ignition coils were fitted in the centre section, over the oil filter. The engine breathed through a single carburettor but this was changed from Amal 363 to Amal Type 19 on later models.

The front fork was the same as the LE but the handlebar rake was adjustable and both gearshift and rear brake pedals worked through holes in the body.

Priced at £246 in 1966, the Vogue was in a class of its own. It was neither a car nor a bike yet it was a bit of both. Its engine pushed out only 8bhp at 5000 rpm and a low centre of gravity contributed to fantastic handling.

While the Vogue won unstinting praise from all who tried it, this unusual Velo went down as one of the classics that didn't make it. Only ten were sold during the last six months of its comparatively short life. A 350 motor might have made all the difference.

OWNER'S STORY

Runs like magic and can make 105 miles on one gallon

Don Thompson is a Velo fan who gets a kick from telling admirers that the Vogue he rides to work was built long before Japanese manufacturers became noise conscious.

"People can't believe a British bike made in 1966 can be so quiet or so modern," says this chemical plant chargehand from Boothstown, near Manchester. "I had to make a small screen because the old one broke long ago. The screen is the only part that is not original.

"The bike runs like magic and cost me £200. It was registered in Hazel Grove, Cheshire, and had three previous owners. It was in reasonable condition but the tank leaked. It took me about a fortnight to strip the body and glue the cracks up. Being in the chemical business helped.

"The forks were so stiff that the bike sprang up the road like a kangaroo. Topping up with oil made all the difference. Inflating the tyres harder than recommended also improved the navigation. I'd ridden an LE before but I did not expect the Vogue to handle as well. It is a really fantastic road holder. You can ride it hands off any time.

"I rebuilt another Vogue for a friend with whom I did a 250 mile trip to Yorkshire and Cumbria. We flew up the one in four Barbon Hill climb in second gear.

"The bike originally had a wire toggle for a choke on the side of the bike. I've glued the wire to the tickler as I find this is quite enough for starting in cold weather.

"On a long run, I get 105mpg but the average is 90mpg. Oil capacity is only two pints, which means a pint every 300 miles, but I haven't put a drop of water in the radiator since I rebuilt the bike."

A Velocette specialist since he discarded a Norton Commando because the seat was too high, Mr Thompson also owns a 500 Thruxton, two LE Velos and a BSA Gold Star.

A 1965 publicity shot emphasised the Vogue's all-weather runabout image. Price at this time was £246.

Specification — Velocette Vogue

ENGINE: Water cooled, horizontally opposed twin cylinder, side valve four-stroke. Bore and stroke 50mm x 49mm. Capacity 192cc. Lightweight alloy heads. Amal 363 carburettor.

TRANSMISSION: Multi-plate dry clutch. Shaft Drive. Velocette four-speed footchange gearbox integral with engine.

ELECTRICS: 6 volt Miller or 12 volt Lucas versions with alternator. Twin 6in. headlamps.

CAPACITIES: 2½ gallons petrol, 1¾ pints oil.

EQUIPMENT: Kickstarter, dualseat, windshield, built-in legshields, glove boxes, footboards, panniers and direction indicators.

WHEELS: Steel rims with fabricated full-width hubs. Tyres 3.25 x 18in front and rear.

BRAKES: 5in single leading shoe drums front and rear.

SUSPENSION: Telescopic front fork, coil springs at rear.

WEIGHT: 275lbs.

MANUFACTURERS: Veloce Ltd, York Road, Hall Green, Birmingham.

Velocette Thruxton

Fast enough to have won a Production TT, the Velocette Thruxton was a hand-built superbike which recaptured some of the racing glories of the Hall Green, Birmingham, factory.

Probably the fastest 500 pushrod single ever made, it was a highly tweaked version of the Venom which hoisted the 500cc world record for 24 hours to over 100mph.

Successes of the Thruxton, named after a circuit famous for long distance production bike racing, included first and second place for Neil Kelly and Keith Heckles in the 1967 TT.

Specification — Velocette Thruxton

ENGINE: Air cooled, single cylinder, overhead valve, pushrod four stroke. Bore and stroke 86mm x 86mm. Capacity 499cc. Compression ratio 9 to 1. Iron cylinder. Alloy head. Amal TT carburettor.

TRANSMISSION: Inboard multi-plate clutch in oil. Single roller primary and secondary chains. Overall ratios (standard) 10.1, 6.97, 5.3 and 4.41 to 1; (TT) 8.4, 6.3, 4.8 and 4.4 to 1.

ELECTRICS: Lucas competition magneto with manual advance and retard. Miller or Lucas dynamo with 6 volt 13 amp hour battery for lights. 7in headlamp.

CAPACITIES: 3 gallons petrol, 4 pints oil.

EQUIPMENT: Kickstarter, dualseat with tail hump, rev-counter, centre and prop stands.

WHEELS: Steel rims (alloy extra) with alloy hubs. Tyres 3.25 x 19in front and rear.

BRAKES: 7½in. front drum, 7in. rear.

SUSPENSION: Veloce telescopic front fork (moto cross pattern) with hydraulic damping. Swinging arm rear springing with Woodhead Monroe or Girling shockers adjustable for load.

DIMENSIONS: Seat height 30½in, ground clearance 5½in, wheelbase 53¾in, overall length 84in, weight 375lbs.

MANUFACTURERS: Veloce Ltd, York Road, Hall Green, Birmingham.

Thoroughbred Velocette Thruxton converted to touring trim, discarding clip-on bars and rear-set footrests.

Although old-fashioned in many ways, the Thruxton punched out almost 46bhp at 6,700rpm.

When it came out, in 1964, the Thruxton cost £369. The price went up to £530 before the last batch was built in December 1970. The Veloce factory went into liquidation in 1971.

In full racing trim, with megaphone exhaust and Isle of Man gearing (3.5 to 1 top) this ton-up mile-eater was reckoned to be good for around 130mph! On standard top gear of 4.7 to 1 (close or wide ratios were available) it was still capable of speeds between 110 and 115mph. And yet the engine and four-speed box were direct descendants of the 1935 MSS!

The original long stroke 495cc MSS (81 x 96mm) went out in 1949. The MSS was revived in 1954 with an all-alloy "square" 499cc (86mm x 86mm). The Venom, with enclosed hairpin valve springs and taper roller main bearings, was introduced in 1958.

Unashamedly old fashioned, with a timing cover identical to the 1935 design, the Thruxton boasted a two-inch inlet valve, a 1⅜ inch Amal GP carburettor, and a 10.8 to 1 compression ratio. It punched out a claimed 45.8bhp at 6700rpm and was noted for uncanny smoothness and free-revving qualities.

Although the low geared kickstarter required a special technique which is part and parcel of the vintage charm of any Velo single, road handling of the Venom was first class.

Easily identified by the prefix VMT for engine numbers, compared with VM for Venom and MSS for the cooking model, the Thruxton came with a swept back exhaust and fishtail silencer modified for extra clearance when cranked over. Other features included a tank cutaway for the GP carb, a Lucas competition magneto, Dunlop alloy rims and a twin leading shoe front brake.

The battery was enclosed in a metal case adopted from the Valiant flat twin and the hump back racing seat was in keeping with clip-ons and rear sets and racing cockpit fairing supplied as original equipment.

OWNER'S STORY

Faults are cancelled by superb handling

Eddie Faulkner, PRO of the Velocette Owners Club, is better known as the owner of an immaculate Velo Valiant which has twice won him the concours at BMF rallies.

But the bike collection of this Northampton toy factory engineer includes a rare example of a Velo Thruxton converted to touring trim.

"I've done 11,000 miles on the Thruxton since I bought it in 1976. I was first in the queue, gave £400 for it and rode it back from Southend in pouring rain.

"I swore then to do away with the clip-ons but arm and backache were not my only problems. The front brake was oval and the lights kept going out. After checking the battery and wiring, I found the dynamo belt was slipping.

"Six volt lighting was always poor on Velos. I have fitted a 12 volt John Gardner electronic conversion. It was well worth the £20 which enabled me to discard the old Miller regulator.

"Oil leaks from crankcase and primary case are a bugbear but this is offset by superb road holding. I once owned a Norton Dominator and my Thruxton handles better.

"In its present form, the Thruxton is both comfortable and practical. The Avon fairing was designed for the MSS, Venom or Viper — and the Craven panniers complete the touring specification."

"I chipped my ankle bone learning the correct starting drill and the clip-ons which were still fitted when I took my father to the 1976 TT, were sheer murder," added Mr Faulkner, whose 1966 Thruxton was originally registered in Southampton.

An enthusiast who has twice scored maximum marks in the ACU's national rally, Mr Faulkner has been a Velo fan since he was an apprentice toolmaker. "I could only afford bikes like Francis Barnetts but I have never been keen on two strokes," he says.

Today, a Thruxton can fetch between £1000 and £1300. And spares for Velocettes are generally cheaper than for any other make on the road.

"The only parts I've had to replace have been one complete clutch, one clutch thrust bearing and a gearbox mainshaft with two gears which shattered.

"I have fitted stainless steel oil and petrol pipes. The only other replacements have been tyres and brake linings. My next job is adjusting a slipping clutch. And that's another Velo ritual!"

Besides his Thruxton, Mr Faulkner has two Velo Valiants in running order and three more in bits. He also has a Venom and a Viper in various stages of restoration.

"Valiant spares are hard to get. I've even had to send off to America for pistons originally made in England," says Mr Faulkner, whose concours winning gem was once a rusty heap.

Introduced in 1956, the 200cc Velo flat twin sported an aircooled engine and shaft drive. It ran like a little turbine, possessed quite lively acceleration, and handled even better than big Velos. Top speed was about 68mph but petrol consumption was in the region of 95 miles to the gallon.

Vincent HRD Rapide

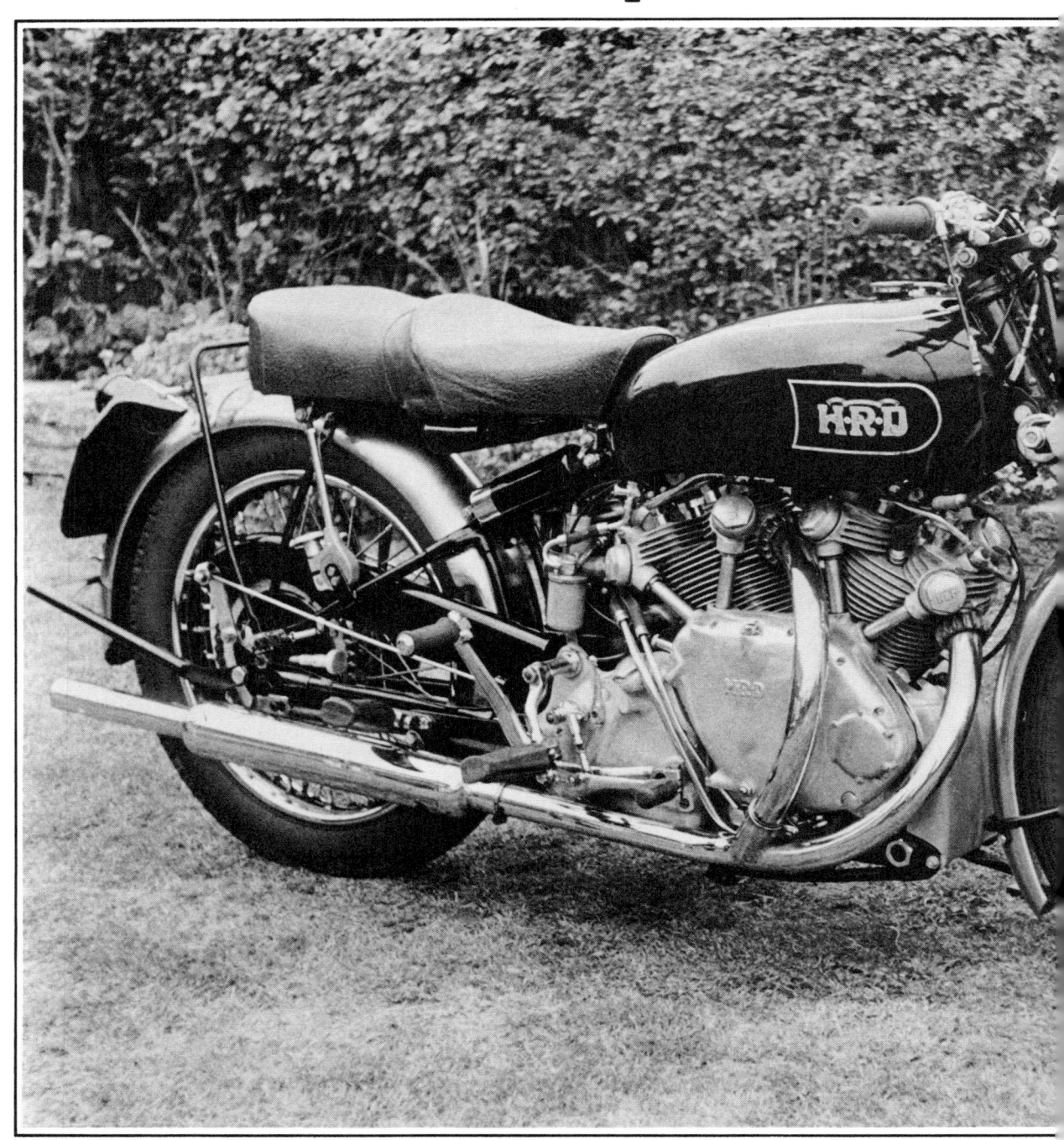

Brainchild of Phil Vincent, who designed his basic cantilever spring frame as a public schoolboy before studying engineering at Cambridge and buying a company liquidated by former TT rider Howard Raymond Davies, the Vincent HRD was the greatest of British superbikes.

A unique machine with a performance only recently matched by Japanese multis in terms of speed, the mighty twin from a modest factory at Stevenage, Hertfordshire, shone with practical features like a back wheel which could be removed in 30 seconds!

Specification — Vincent HRD Rapide

ENGINE: Air cooled, 50 degree V-twin cylinder, pushrod, overhead valve four stroke. Bore and stroke 84mm x 90mm. Capacity 998cc. Compression ratio 6.45 to 1. Alloy cylinders with iron liners. Alloy heads with iron valve inserts. Amal carburettors.

TRANSMISSION: Servo clutch, triplex primary chain, single row rear chain. Four-speed gearbox in unit with engine. Overall ratios 9.1, 5.5, 4.16 and 3.5 to 1.

ELECTRICS: Lucas magneto ignition. Manual advance and retard. Miller 50 watt dynamo and 6 volt 13 amp hour battery lighting. 8in headlamp.

CAPACITIES: 3½ gallons petrol, 6 pints oil in frame tank.

EQUIPMENT: Kickstarter, rear and side stands, dualseat, aluminium mudguards, pillion pegs.

WHEELS: Steel rims with pull out spindles. Tyres 3.00 x 20in. front, 3.50 x 19in. rear.

BRAKES: Dual 7in. drums front and rear with compensated leverage. Fulcrum adjusters.

SUSPENSION: Brampton girder front forks, cantilever rear springing with enclosed spring boxes under seat.

DIMENSIONS: Seat height 30in, ground clearance 5in, wheelbase 56½in, overall length 86½in, weight 455lbs.

MANUFACTURERS: Vincent HRD Co Ltd, Stevenage, Hertfordshire.

A late 1949 Series B Rapide

The 998cc (84mm x 90mm) pushrod V-twin engine of the Vincent HRD Series B Rapide, introduced in 1946, has a claimed power output of only 45bhp at 5300rpm but a top gear of 3.5 to 1 made it deceptively fast.

It was capable of 110mph. And high gearing and good handling made it gobble the miles without apparent effort.

Along, with fellow designer Phil Irving, an Australian who made important contributions to the extraordinary personality of hand-built Vincents — the initials HRD were dropped on later models — Mr Vincent devoted his life to making a better bike than anybody else.

His machines always had four brakes. And although the drums of a Rapide were only seven inchers, braking distance of 28 feet from 30mph became the yard-stick by which others were judged.

Developed from the Series A Rapide of 1936, a ferocious beast with a nasty habit of shearing the

V-twin majesty from Vincent. Machine on the opposite page is a 1939 Series A.

gears and burning the clutch of its Burman box, the Series B sported Vincent's integral gearbox, capable of transmitting 200bhp, and a servo clutch like an expanding brake.

Details included Brampton girder forks, replaced by Vincent Girdraulics on later models, a complex gear pedal abbreviated on C and D versions, and the very first dualseat!

Seat stays on the cantilever back end were also friction shock absorbers, a pair of plain springs in metal cases under the seat being the only suspension until a hydraulic damper was sandwiched between them on the Series C.

The grandfather of all kick-starters and ingenious valve gear were features of the big twins which reigned from 1946 to 1956 (Vincent bought HRD in 1928) but their true hallmark was a disappearing back wheel and a breed of affluent riders who rode bow-legged with straight arms close together.

OWNER'S STORY

How would Vincents be today if still in business?

A car body repairer from Kettering, Northants, Tony Wilson, gets more pleasure from tinkering with his Vincents than from bending the elbow in his local.

Owner of six Vincent HRDs, he has made his hobby an extension of his work. "I rebuild my wheels, make oil and petrol tanks, and anything else I can make more cheaply than buying it," he says.

Currently rebuilding a 1951 Series C Black Shadow which he acquired as a load of bits and painstakingly re-enamelled, Mr Wilson acquired his first Vincent HRD in 1958.

"I gave £7 10s for it. It was a fair price in those days and is worth a lot more now. It is a 1934 Model J, with one of the JAP engines which proved so unreliable at the TT that Phil Vincent decided to build his own. But even in those days his bikes had four brakes.

"The famous straight bars were introduced for the 1935 TT. As they had cantilever suspension from the very start, it is interesting to speculate what a Vincent would be like today if the factory hadn't gone broke.

"I came back to bikes four years ago. I don't go very fast on the Series B, with my son Nigel generally on the back, but it does 60 miles to the gallon at 60mph.

"The engine tends to be a bit clattery but you don't hear it over 40. It is completely effortless to ride and will pull top gear down to 25mph.

"Although the compression ratio is only 7 to 1 — they were originally only 6.8 to 1 for petrol not much better than paraffin — it will still do 100mph without any trouble.

"Even my pre-war Series A will do up to 90 on half throttle. It took me six months to cure all the oil leaks. It was a plumber's nightmare. The post-war bikes were much tidier and cleaner."

Vincent Black Shadow

The world's fastest standard production motor cycle when it was launched in 1948, the legendary Vincent Black Shadow continued to reign supreme long after the Stevenage factory closed in 1955.

Built by idealists and aimed at an exclusive set rich enough to afford the best, the Shadow was the first touring bike with a 100mph touring speed and a top whack of more than two miles a minute.

While a maximum of 125 to 130mph may not seem exceptional by today's superbike standards, it must be remembered that all this was when British motorways and Japanese bikes were unheard of.

To a generation of riders weaned on high revs and disc brakes, it may seem equally incredible that the Shadow's puny-looking drum brakes were capable of stopping the bike from 30mph in only 22 feet 6 inches. The bike was fitted with four brakes, as were all Vincents, but although early Shadows had girder forks, the Series C version sported the famous Girdraulics which became synonymous with the technical superiority of the marque.

One of many innovations with which engineering wizards Phil Vincent and Phil Irving attracted fastidious enthusiasts, the forks were superior to both girders and telescopics. Combining girder geometry with the comfort of a conventional telescope layout, the forks were stronger, stiffer and a lot more expensive than the more popular alternatives.

Each fork leg was a light alloy forging with eccentrics on the bottom links to which the fork springs were attached. These eccentrics gave instant trail and spring rate adjustment for solo and sidecar work while a central hydraulic unit took care of damping.

The bike bristled with practical novelty. Such features would still delight today's riders but they would probably drive Japanese cost accountants to drink.

Remember that the Shadow was built regardless of cost and that the price new was in the region of a year's salary for a rider with a skilled trade.

Tommy bars on both wheels enabled really rapid removal and the only tool necessary was a pair of pliers to detach the spring clip of the rear chain. The whole back end could be removed more quickly than the rear wheel of many modern machines. Finger adjusters for both brake and chain tension were other refinements in a specification which included a full range of settings for handlebars, footrests and gear and brake pedals.

More potent version of the Rapide, the Shadow was powered by a tweaked-up 998cc vee-twin en-

Virtually as new in its all-black livery, this Black Shadow is an outstanding example of a superlative machine.

gine (84 x 90mm bore and stroke) with highly polished flywheels, ports, combustion chambers, valve rockers and con rods, high compression pistons, high lift cams, and bigger carburettors.

It had cantilever rear suspension on taper roller bearings but virtually no frame, the massive engine and gearbox unit forming an anchorage for the front and back ends. The only component which could be described as a frame was a steel box from the steering head to the rear spring and damper units. And that steel box acted as an oil tank.

The effortless manner in which the Shadow made a meal of German autobahns and American highways is reflected in a claimed power output of 55bhp at only 5,700rpm. The engine was a slow-revver which made the Shadow deceptively fast. Pulling a

Deceptively fast, the Black Shadow would manage today's legal speed limit at a fast tickover.

Specification — Vincent Black Shadow

ENGINE: Air cooled, 50 degree V-twin, pushrod, overhead valve four stroke. Bore and stroke 84mm x 90mm. Capacity 998cc. Compression ratio 7.3 to 1. Alloy cylinders with iron liners. Alloy heads with iron valve inserts. Amal carburettors.

TRANSMISSION: Servo clutch, triplex primary chain, single row rear chain. Integral four-speed gearbox. Overall ratios 7.2, 5.64, 4.16 and 3.5 to 1.

ELECTRICS: Lucas magneto ignition. Manual advance/retard. Miller 50 watt dynamo and 6 volt 13 amp hour Exide battery. 7in. headlamp.

CAPACITIES: 3½ gallons petrol, 6 pints oil in frame tank.

EQUIPMENT: Kickstarter, exhaust valve lifters, rear and side stands, dualseat, aluminium mudguards, 5in. 150mph Smiths speedo.

WHEELS: Steel rims, ribbed hub castings with pull out spindles. Tyres 3.00 x 20in front, 3.50 x 19in. rear.

BRAKES: Dual 7in. drums front and rear with compensated leverage. Fulcrum adjusters.

SUSPENSION: Vincent Girdraulic front fork. Cantilever rear springing with twin enclosed springs under seat.

DIMENSIONS: Seat height 30in, ground clearance 5in, wheelbase 56½in, overall length 85½in, weight 457lbs.

MANUFACTURERS: Vincent Engineers (Stevenage) Ltd., Stevenage, Hertfordshire.

3.5 top gear, the bike would rustle along at today's legal limit at little more than a fast tickover but the pride and joy of Shadow owners was the biggest and most accurate speedo in the business. With a five-inch dial calibrated to 150mph, and mounted almost vertically for legibility, the special Smiths instrument became the most famous speedometer ever made.

A passion for perfection was reflected in the construction of the black-enamelled engine which formed the basis for the highly tuned Black Lightning of which no more than 20 examples were produced. George Brown, one of the conspirators associated with the original development of the Shadow, used a super-charged Lightning to set several world records in the 'fifties and 'sixties.

OWNER'S STORY

Restored by ex-Vincent men to "as new"

A former despatch rider in the German army who settled in Britain after the war, Karl Birke could not afford a Black Shadow when he rode motor cycles by necessity.

Now a garage proprietor, at Baldock, Herts, he has an impressive collection of British bikes and a 1954 Shadow, one of the last to be built at nearby Stevenage, enjoys pride of place.

"I've only done about 50 miles on it since it was completely restored. Quite frankly, I'm afraid of dropping it," says Mr Birke. I have been accused of hoarding machines which younger men should be riding but, if it were not for people like me, classic motor cycles like the Shadow could cease to exist.

"When I first came here, I got to know some of the people at the Vincent factory. I always yearned to have one but they were beyond my pocket. The first time I actually owned a Vincent was when I bought a 1951 500 Comet. I then got bitten by the bug and the Shadow was a natural progression.

"Ted Davies, a former Vincent factory tester, got the Shadow for me. It was in restorable condition but it is now virtually brand new. The work was carried out by Jack Furnace and Alf Searle, two former Vincent employees who now specialise in restoring these machines at Cromer, Hertfordshire.

"My first peacetime bike was a 500 Matchless in 1949 but I have always been a motor cycling enthusiast. My wife and I did many happy miles with an old Harley and my latest acquisition is a 1939 SS80 Brough Superior sidecar outfit."

Mr Birke also has an Ariel Square Four, a Red Hunter, a Scott Squirrel and treasures an intriguing memento of his military initiation to two wheels — a 250 DKW used by the Russian army after the war.

Vincent Comet 500

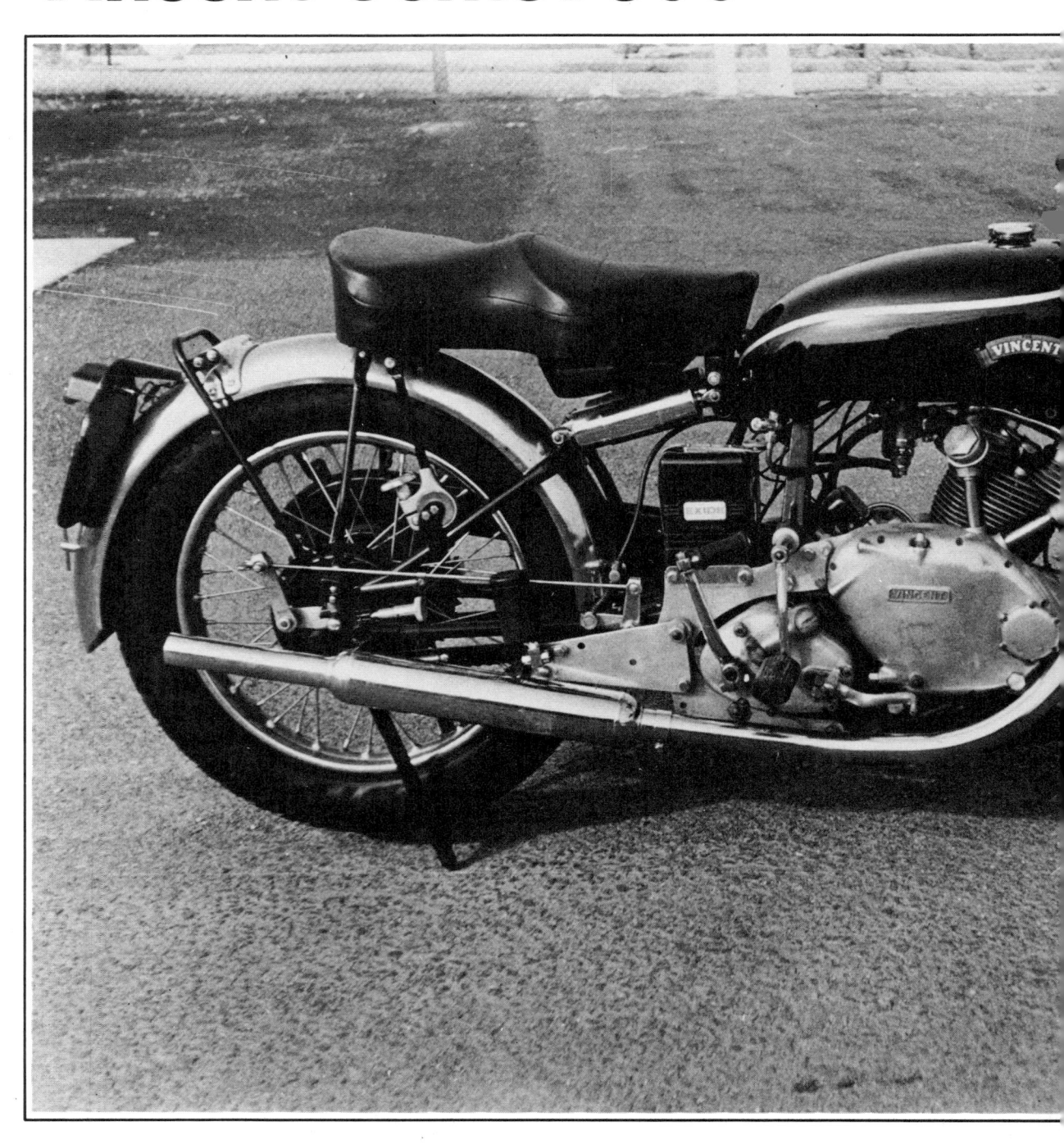

Virtually half a Vincent twin, the 500 Series C Comet was a real cracker which, to many enthusiasts, still represents the ultimate in single cylinder hardware.

The faster it was ridden the better it handled, being good for nearly 90mph. It was fairly heavy but it had incredibly good brakes. And the tonk-tonk-tonk of its exhaust was sheer magic.

It had such a ring of quality that, if a Japanese factory announced an updated version with 12 volt electrics tomorrow, there would probably be a waiting list overnight.

Outstanding by any standards, the post-war Comet was a logical development of the high camshaft, short pushrod singles successfully raced by Vincent HRD before World War Two.

The most obvious difference was an inclined instead of upright cylinder. The alloy barrel, inclined at 25 degrees, was interchangeable with those of a Vincent V-twin. And the bottom half was almost a carbon copy.

The engine's remarkable smoothness stemmed largely from its beefy crankshaft. The assembly was as strong as that of a Rapide but with the main bearings closer together.

The strength of this bottom half was evident when, some 30 years after the Comet was introduced at Earls Court, Brian Chapman hurtled his Mighty Mouse 500cc dragster over a standing start quarter mile in less than nine seconds.

Although later fitted with a con-rod from a Manx Norton, Chapman's supercharged sprinter running on nitro retained the original bottom-end of a touring Comet. His output was 120bhp. His terminal speed 156mph!

Of the 820 pre-war Comets with vertical engines built between 1934 and 1939, only a few were actually raced but notable TT riders included Jack Williams. Jock West and Manliffe Barrington.

Post-war Vincent factory records are not renowned for their accuracy but approximately 2,000 Series C Comets, and their derivatives, were built from 1948 to 1954 when the model was discontinued.

Only a handful of Meteor versions were produced, the Series B being available from 1948 until 1950 with an identical 499cc (84mm x 90mm bore and stroke) engine but a lower compression ratio.

Last of the line was the Series D Victor with full enclosure. Only one of these machines was built, in 1954, but there was also one example of a Series D Comet with exposed engine.

Like its more powerful brethren, the Comet did

The ultimate in single cylinder hardware?

Virtually half a Vincent twin, the 500 had a 25 degree inclined cylinder and was noted for remarkable smoothness. Barrels were interchangeable between singles and twins and there was little difference in the bottom half.

Specification — Vincent Comet 500

ENGINE: Air cooled, single cylinder, pushrod, overhead valve four stroke. Bore and stroke 84mm x 90mm. Capacity 499cc. Compression ratio: 6.8 to 1. Triple valve springs. Alloy barrel and head. Amal 1 1/8 inch carburettor.

TRANSMISSION: Multi-plate clutch running in oil. Single roller primary and secondary chains. Burman four-speed footchange gearbox. Overall ratios 12.4, 8.17, 5.94 and 4.64 to 1.

ELECTRICS: Lucas magneto ignition. Miller 36 watt dynamo. Exide 6 volt 13 amp hour battery 7in headlamp.

CAPACITIES: 3½ gallons petrol, 6 pints oil in frame tank.

EQUIPMENT: Kickstarter, exhaust valve lifter, dualseat, prop and rear stands, pillion footrests.

WHEELS: Quickly detachable, interchangeable, with steel rims and pull out spindles. Tyres 3.00 x 20in. front, 3.50 x 19in. rear.

SUSPENSION: Vincent Girdraulic front fork. Cantilever rear springing with twin enclosed springs under seat.

DIMENSIONS: Seat height 30in, ground clearance 6in, wheelbase 56in, overall length 85½in, weight 390lbs.

MANUFACTURERS: Vincent Engineers (Stevenage) Ltd, Stevenage, Herts.

not sport a normal frame. Instead, it had a box-section top member, which also served as an oil tank. The engine and a cast alloy pillar completed the sprung portion of the machine.

Unlike the twins, the transmission included a single row primary chain (¼in. x 5/16in.) to a multi-plate clutch and four-speed Burman gearbox with a longer than standard mainshaft to align with the engine.

The Burman internals were similar to those of an AJS or Matchless box but the casing had a single pivot bolt at the top and an adjustment slot at the bottom.

The Comet was not a high revver. At 70mph in top it was tonking over at around 4,000rpm. But it would go to nearly 7,000 when tweaked to nearly 70mph in second.

Dual brakes front and rear, along with Girdraulic forks and cantilever rear springing, were retained on the Grey Flash racing version developed by George and Cliff Brown in 1949. About 30 were built and one was raced by John Surtees during his apprenticeship at Stevenage.

Although all bike production stopped in 1955, the company survived as Vincent Engineers (Stevenage) Ltd., until 1959. It then became Harper Engines Ltd and the Vincent part of the business was sold to Velocette in 1975.

OWNER'S STORY

Electrics the weakness

Paul Newman, a civil engineering student whose first bike was saved from the dust cart, restored his 1951 Series C Vincent Comet before he was old enough to ride it.

Only seven when he gave a dustman two shillings for a 50cc Corgi scooter which he later sprinted at Duxford, he was just 16 when he bought the Comet in a dilapidated condition in 1973.

"It was pretty rough. It was originally sold by Jack Surtees, whose bronze nameplate it still carries, but the Comet went from London to owners in Birmingham and Manchester before I got it. I gave £195 to become the fifth owner. My aim was to make it outshine my father's Rapide," he said.

Bill Newman, owner of a Series C Rapide since 1959, gave his son a little help but Paul undertook most of the work himself and paid for bits from part-time jobs.

"The worst was preparing parts for finishing. I couldn't afford to replace all nuts and bolts so I got rid of the scratches and trimmed the faces on a lathe.

"As I polished them myself the cost of cadmium plating was minimal. Stove enamelling started in my mother's kitchen. When she disapproved of the smell I got an old oven and enlarged it."

In 1977, father and son took their bikes to the Vincent HRD owners rally, near Shadow Lake, Ontario, Canada, carrying out a makeshift repair when the Comet's valve lifter pulled of a cable nipple.

Paul has since rebuilt a 1970 500 Honda-four for daily transport.

"The Comet isn't too easy to keep clean, and night riding can be a bit dodgy," says the budding dam and tunnel builder.

"The six-volt electrics are the weakest point. Output of the Miller dynamo is only 36 watts which is well under the total taken by head, tail, speedo and stop lights."

Owners Club Directory

AJS and Matchless Owners Club

The AJS and Matchless Owners Club caters for about a thousand enthusiasts, including many overseas members. There are 16 branches in Britain and an independent organisation in Holland.

Established in 1952, the club made a nostalgic trip to the Isle of Man 26 years later. Matchless founder Charlie Collyer won the single cylinder class of the first TT back in 1907 and Rod Coleman gave the combined marque its last victory in the 1954 Junior with a triple knocker 350 7R AJS.

Jampot is the monthly magazine for members and main event in the calendar is a Jampot Rally, held around August Bank Holiday each year. A series of four stroke trials have been successfully staged since 1977.

While spares for some models are still relatively easy to obtain, the club is hoping to link with Vincent owners to manufacture problem parts. Spares organiser is chairman Keith Jackson, 49 Sandringham Drive, Spondon, Derby, backed by five officers dealing with specific categories.

For membership details contact secretary Robert Pearce, 132 Shenstone Avenue, Stourbridge, West Midlands.

Ariel Owners MCC

Started by a group of Ariel fans meeting at the Ace Cafe, on the outskirts of London, Ariel Owners MCC has been in operation since 1951. It now has over 1,000 members from almost every country in the world while Britain is covered by 17 branches.

Like the majority of one-make clubs it is affiliated to the BMF. A busy calendar includes rallies, long distance runs and social functions. A monthly magazine, Cheval de Fer (Horse of Iron) goes to all members.

The club took over many spares when the Ariel factory closed and these are handled by four spares organisers, separately covering two-strokes, singles, twins and the Square Four. A large range of regalia is also available.

Secretary is motor cycle shop owner Mick Stroud, St. Hilary, Helmdon Road, Sulgrave, Nr. Banbury, Oxon.

BSA Owners Club

With some 2,000 members from practically every country in the world, the BSA Owners' Club is a truly international organisation dedicated to keeping the products of Birmingham Small Arms alive.

Most members own more than one machine. In the East Midlands one enthusiast from Northampton has a collection of no fewer than 19 BSAs. And most members ride and maintain their historic specimens.

Originally founded in Sheffield, in 1958, the club expanded so rapidly that, by 1960, there were branches a few miles apart with different aims, rules and even membership fees.

In 1963, a national club was formed which ironed out these differences. The "national" tag was dropped in 1970, because of growing overseas involvement, and the original social and competitive activities have expanded tremendously.

For details of 20 British branches contact secretary Barry "Polly" Palmer, 244 The Cullerns, Haresfield, Highworth, Swindon, Wilts SN6 7NL.

Gold Star Owners Club

Such is the charisma of the BSA Gold Star that, in addition to the BSA Owners Club, a separate organisation thrives for devotees of these attractive singles.

The Gold Star Owners Club, which also caters for Rocket GS enthusiasts, has over 300 members in Britain and approximately the same number in the USA, recalling the hey-days when Goldies were raced at Daytona, BSA produced short circuit versions for the USA, and also built a special Catalina scrambler.

There are eight branches throughout the country which hold regular meetings and the club is setting up its own magazine to replace the imported American one. Main function of the year is a two-day rally.

A spares scheme is run by chairman Jim Gardner, 23 Wellington Close, Dibdon Purlieu, Nr. Southampton, Hants. A good range of parts is available, manufactured mainly by companies that used to supply BSA.

Secretary is John Corble, Southwold, Moor Lane, Sherburn-in-Elmet, North Yorkshire.

London Douglas MCC

One of the prime aims of London Douglas MCC is to expand its already impressive spares service for Douglas owners. Parts are salvaged and manufactured, but it is the range of new components that club officers realise must be expanded to keep alive a marque that ended in 1957.

The club was formed in 1928 when Douglas sports machines were dominant, giving rise to the motto Facile Princeps — always to the fore. Today it has several sections in Britain plus many overseas members, particularly in New Zealand and Australia.

A magazine, the New Conrod, keeps enthusiasts informed and provides a medium for the exchange of practical advice on the many machines still in everyday use. Douglas (Sales and Service) continues under club vice president Eric Brockway, proud owner of a 500 prototype built in 1952. The firm currently imports Vespa scooters and Gilera motorcycles.

Membership secretary is Mr J Rogers, Bryn Dinas, Nant Gwynant, Caernarvon, Gwynedd.

Norton Owners Club

Formed in 1955, the Norton Owners Club has grown to 12 branches in Britain and four in the USA, Holland and Czechoslovakia, where many Nortons were sold after World War Two. Membership is about 1,200 owners.

Associate membership is available for people who do not have a local branch. A monthly magazine "Roadholder" helps owners to get spares and to attend events. The club also runs technical advice and emergency help schemes and in 1977 negotiated the manufacture of rare spares at special rates.

An annual rally is the highlight of a busy programme. Secretary is Peter Thistle, 30 Rosehill Avenue, Sutton, Surrey.

Panther Owners Club

The Panther Owners Club — not to be confused with the separate older Panther and Associate Sidecar Club — was formed in the Spring of 1976 out of the Midlands Panther Club, then a year old and 80 members strong.

The name was changed to promote a national image, and the role of the club is to keep the marque on the road as a reliable, regular form of transport.

Membership has now grown to well over 300 all over the world. There's a monthly magazine 'Sloper', a breakdown scheme, and the club organises rallies and camping weekends all over Britain.

But perhaps the most important aspect of POC activities is the comprehensive spares scheme with three spares secretaries and a co-ordinating sub-committee to determine demand and manufacturing priorities.

Manufacture of spares is undoubtedly the key to the club's continued success and a workshop manual is being written. It's the club's aim to make sure there is always enough spares to keep the machines of all its members on the road.

For details contact Steve Rogers, 36 Coombe Road, Croydon, Surrey.

Royal Enfield Owners Club

The Royal Enfield Owners Club is enjoying a second lease of life. Originally founded in the early 1950s, it folded along with the factory and was only revived in 1977 to cope with renewed interest in the marque.

Membership has grown steadily to over 300 with new branches appearing all over the country. Owners from Paris are often seen at club rallies and social events. Newsletters are sent out every two months but a quarterly magazine, The Gun, is now established.

Virtually all spares still available are shared between Gander and Gray, Manor Park, London E12; E and S Motors, Chiswick, London W4; and L and D Motors, Bristol. They work closely with the club.

More recently new components have been manufactured, including reproduction chain cases in glass fibre, seat covers and pans, and Airflow fairings, produced from a mould that social secretary Steve Bucknall took from an original.

Secretary is Don McKeand, 15 Grove Road, Dunstable, Beds.

Scott Owners Club

Founded in 1958, the Scott Owners Club is a lively organisation with branches as far as America, Australia, New Zealand and South Africa.

The president is Harold Scott, nephew of the man who gave the world a machine that was truly different.

Monthly gatherings are held by six British branches, the club keeps an accurate register, publishes a very informative magazine called Yowl, and organises a number of national rallies.

Secretary is Mrs S Cumming, 22 Brendon Avenue, Chamberlain Road, Hull, North Humberside.

Sunbeam Fellowship

The Sunbeam Fellowship was formed in 1962 by a breakaway group from the Sunbeam Club, which was then mainly a sporting organisation. Membership has grown to around 300, typically spanning many different countries. There's even one enthusiast in India.

Chairman is Bob Stewart, whose company Stewart

Engineering, Sunbeam Works, Disraeli Road, Putney, London SW15, is the only firm left still producing spares for Sunbeam machines. Stewart's can supply most items and an indication of how many bikes are still running around the world is given by a sale of over 4,000 modified breathing covers.

Membership is not restricted to owners of Sunbeams and it entitles you to the Fellowship's bi-monthly magazine, On the Beam. Social highlights are an annual rally and autojumble.

For details, write to "Rotor", c/o Stewart Engineering.

Triumph Owners MCC

One of Britain's largest one-make clubs, the Triumph Owners MCC was formed in 1949. It now has seventeen branches with overseas sections in America, France and Sweden.

The club is significantly stronger than at any time before, with around 1,500 members. Even during Triumph's peak years membership was never more than about the 1,300 mark.

A sporting section promotes high speed trials and racing at Lydden while a number of rallies are now established in the calendar of national social activities. Branches also carry out their own programmes.

A monthly magazine, Nacelle — "written by the members for the members" — records news and information. But the club's biggest headache is spares, despite the co-operation of many dealers and Meriden Motor Cycles.

General secretary is Eddie Foulkes, Tye View, Honey Tye, Leavenheath, Colchester, Essex. Membership, and many other areas of administration, are the responsibility of assistant secretary Edna Page, 101 Great Knightleys, Basildon, Essex, whose husband, Harry, is club president and treasurer.

Velocette Owners Club

Soaring membership has made the Velocette Owners Club a very strong organisation indeed. Even with the condition that applicants must own, or have owned, a Velocette, there are around 1,700 enthusiasts on the books plus a large number of associate members.

The club was founded in 1957 at the Red House pub, Park Road, London NW8. There are now 25 centres worldwide with strong groups in Canada and Holland. Run for riders rather than collectors, Velocette OC produces its own 64-page magazine, Fishtail, every six weeks and promotes an annual national rally at Stanford Hall.

Spares for post-war Velos are still relatively cheap and easy to obtain, produced by the Velocette Motorcycle Company and distributed through about a dozen dealers. To cater for older machines, the club set up Veloce Spares Ltd, under the control of Jim Plant. You have to be a member to get the benefit.

Secretary is Alan Wright, 25 Crawley Close, Slip End, Luton, Beds, while applications for membership are handled by Ted Snelling, 3 Hadley Road, Mitcham, Surrey.

Vincent HRD Owners Club

A very professional organisation, the Vincent HRD Owners Club even has its own factory manufacturing parts, though it is run completely independently. The club raised £40,000 from a share issue to establish the works at Lymm, in Cheshire, when the original Vincent business began to run down.

Over thirty sections all over the world boast a membership of around 2,000. The club began in 1948 and president up to his death in 1978 was Phil Vincent.

Social or sporting events take place most weekends and in recent years different countries have hosted international rallies. Members are kept informed through a monthly club magazine, simply called MPH, which has been circulating since 1949.

Secretary is Bill Hancock, 39 Dawson Avenue, Beech Hill, Wigan, Lancs, but for spares service the contact is Robin Blackwell, 170 Havant Road, Hayling Island, Hants. There's also a regalia stockholder for such items as an all-metal model kit and man with the job is Len Matthews, 15 Knox Gardens, Clacton-on-Sea, Essex.

British Motor Cyclists Federation

While all owner's club contacts given here were accurate at the time of going to press, it is possible that some officers or addresses may have changed. A useful guide to motor cycle organisations is updated and published annually by the British Motorcyclists' Federation. Known as the BMF Directory of Clubs, it is available from The British Motorcyclists' Federation, 225 Coventry Road, Ilford, Essex IG1 4RF.

The BMF represents over 20,000 riders and is dedicated to protecting their interests.